Establishing Agreement

Studies of Conversation in Pragmatics and Discourse Analysis (PDA)

This series contains reports on original research in both pragmatics and discourse analysis. Contributions from linguists, philosophers, logicians, cognitive psychologists, and researchers in speech communication are brought together to promote interdisciplinary research into a variety of topics in the study of language use. In this series several kinds of studies are presented under headings such as 'Argumentation', 'Conversation' and 'Interpretation'.

Establishing Agreement

An analysis of proposal-acceptance sequences

Hanneke Houtkoop

1987
FORIS PUBLICATIONS
Dordrecht-Holland/Providence U.S.A.

Published by:
Foris Publications Holland
P.O. Box 509
3300 AM Dordrecht, The Netherlands

Sole distributor for the U.S.A. and Canada:
Foris Publications USA, Inc.
P.O. Box 5904
Providence RI 02903
U.S.A.

CIP-DATA

Houtkoop, Hanneke

Establishing Agreement / Hanneke Houtkoop. – Dordrecht [etc.] : Foris. – (Pragmatics and Discourse Analysis ; 4)
Also published as thesis University of Amsterdam, 1987. – With ref.
ISBN 90-6765-328-4 bound
SISO 305.8 UDC 316.4:371.334
Subject heading: communication.

ISBN 90 6765 328 4

Printed in The Netherlands by ICG Printing, Dordrecht.

for my parents

and

for Gail Jefferson

Contents

1 Introduction

1.1 The research problem

The work to be presented here is the result of the analysis of proposal-acceptance sequences in Dutch telephone conversations. The term 'proposal' refers to a range of actions such as requests, invitations, offers, and the like. They all have in common that by making a proposal the speaker solicits his [1] recipient to agree to carry out the activity under discussion.

What is proposed is to be performed some time after the current conversation: turning up at a party, passing on a piece of information, collaborating in the offered or promised action of the speaker, etc. Such proposals are called here 'proposals for remote action', or 'remote proposals', and they differ from 'immediate proposals' which are proposals to perform some action immediately. In many cases the proposal will turn out to be a request formulated more or less indirectly. (See 1.1.1 for a more extended discussion of 'proposal'.)

A proposal, together with its acceptance, will be considered to be a social action produced collaboratively and interactively in the conversation. Such a social action therefore is seen as being produced as a conversational action. By uttering a proposal and accepting this proposal conversationalists perform the social action of making an arrangement for some action to be carried out, and they perform this social action as a conversational action, i.e. as a proposal sequence.

In this way conversational actions are seen as corresponding to social actions, and each part of a conversational action matches a part of the social action being produced interactively. This perspective particularly plays a role when one looks upon proposal sequences as conversation units which are opened and closed off, and which are markedly distinct from what precedes and follows them in the conversation.

The theoretical framework of the analysis is Conversation Analysis (henceforth CA), as introduced by the late Harvey Sacks, and continued by his students and colleagues Gail Jefferson, Emanuel Schegloff, and others. Much of the work done by CA concerns the sequential organization of conversation.

In the literature such sequences as proposal sequences are considered to be adjacency pairs, i.e. two-part sequences consisting of a proposal as its first pair-part, and the acceptance as its second pair-part. In contrast I will present the proposal sequence as a five-part sequence, consisting of two adjacently positioned adjacency pairs plus a fifth and sequence-closing utterance (see the Appendix for the transcription notations):

proposal	S. But come over here, so we can all talk about it in peace.=
acceptance	R. =Fine.
request-for-confirmation	S. Yah?=
confirmation	R. =I'll be there in a minute.=
acknowledgement	S. =O:kay.

Speaker initiates the sequence by a proposal ("But come over here"), which is accepted by the recipient in second sequence-position ("Fine"). A request-for-confirmation of this acceptance is made ("Yah?"), and when the recipient has produced the solicited confirmation of his preceding acceptance ("I'll be there in a minute"), the speaker closes the collaborative action with a sequence-closing object, often an "Okay". This closing object paves the way for a subsequent new and unrelated action.

This sequence, as produced by the conversationalists, makes it possible to turn an initial proposal into a final arrangement about the performance by the recipient of the action proposed. Recipient is not only willing to carry it out, but also promises to do so as he claims in his fourth-positioned utterance. The sequential structure allows for a potential discussion of the details of the proposed action and its performance.

Once the recipient has initially agreed to the proposal, the speaker may provide further details which are relevant to the performance of the action, and therefore relevant to the final acceptance in the fourth position of the sequence. And before the recipient confirms his acceptance he may ask for further details, or initiate other talk about carrying out the action. This provision is important since the proposal concerns an action the speaker needs to be sure of whether or not it will indeed be adequately carried out. All potential problems and uncertainties need to be solved before the discussion at hand is closed.

In order to be able to discuss these sequences, the following topics will be considered. After an account in Chapter 1 of the data on which this analysis is based, Chapter 2 will deal with the theoretical background of CA, i.e. Ethnomethodology, and several general CA-notions will be outlined. Chapter 3 will be devoted to the sequential approach of CA. In this chapter I will discuss Sacks, Schegloff & Jefferson's model for conversational turn-taking, and the problematic aspects of this model, i.e. the lack of a semantic-pragmatic viewpoint on their turn-taking model. Then the notion of next-positionedness of utterances (i.e. adjacency pairs) will be discussed. Whereas in the CA-literature adjacency pairs are treated as two-part sequences, I will argue that they are basically three-part structures, i.e. 'adjacency triplets' (see 3.3.1). After the recipient has produced the second part of an adjacency pair, there is a strong tendency towards the production of a third utterance produced by the first speaker, by which he assesses the response as satisfactory, and by which he closes the sequence. This sequence-closing utterance is also present in the proposal sequence, the reason for discussing this aspect of adjacency pairs in more detail. Furthermore I will address the preference organization in conversations (see 3.4). Requests, invitations, offers, and such have two alternative response-types, acceptance or rejection, the former preferred to the latter. A rejection has consequences for the turn-shape of the response utterance, and so for the sequence under analysis.

The analysis of the proposal sequence will be presented in Chapter 4. Whereas the immediate proposal sequence is seen as an adjacency triplet (4.1), the remote proposal sequence will be presented as a five-part sequence (4.2). In 4.3 it will be shown that certain responses to the proposal are not fitted for accepting the proposal, and how proposer may react to such 'weak acceptance-forms'. For example, speaker may continue and explain why the proposal is being made, or he may give a candidate analyis of why recipient does not (fully) accept the proposal, or he may prompt a better response. In 4.4 the proposal sequence will be unravelled into its two sequential components, i.e. the proposal/initial acceptance sequence, and the request-for-confirmation/ confirmation sequence. The initial proposal and its acceptance will turn out to be 'interactionally achieved' (4.4.2).

In this first sequence the willingness of the recipient to carry out the proposed action is at stake, and in the second sequence his ability (4.4.3). It will then be shown (4.4.4) that participants demonstrate in various ways that they consider themselves to have made an arrangement with regard to carrying out the proposed action. Since these sequences frequently occur in the closing section of the conversation, 4.5.1.1 discusses the sequence from the perspective of being 'closing implicative'. The fact that proposal sequences easily lead up to conversational closing, or may even be part of the closing itself, is used to explain why these sequences may be cut off before the sequence-closing utterance has been produced.

1.1.1 The subject matter

The object of this research consists of a range of action sequences such as request, invitation, offer, suggestion, plea, and promise sequences. These actions are classed under the general label 'proposals'.

In terms of speech act theory these actions belong to the classes of 'directives' and 'commissives' (Searle 1976). Directives are attempts by the speaker to make the hearer carry out something (Searle 1976:11), for example, requesting, questioning, ordering, advising, pleading, begging, permitting, or inviting. Ervin-Tripp (1981) sees directives as belonging to the larger class of 'control moves' which affect the addressee's actions.

Other authors use different terms for these directive speech acts. To mention some of them: Green (1975) talks about 'impositives', "to cover speech acts, regardless of their form, by which a speaker's desire or opinion is imposed on the addressee as an order, demand, request, plea, warning, or suggestion." (Green 1975:125). Haverkate (1979) makes a distinction between 'impositive directives' which are of interest to the speaker, and 'non-impositive directives' linked with the demands of the addressee (1979:31). Lyons (1977) speaks of 'mands', "utterances which impose, or propose, some course of action or pattern of behaviour and indicate that it should be carried out.", and "other subclasses of directives, such as warnings, recommendations and exhortations." (Lyons 1977:745-6).

With a commissive (Searle 1976) the speaker promises to carry out a future action. Commissives are then, among others, promises and offers. As Hancher (1979) points out, directives and commissives involve cooperation. For example, inviting and offering are commissives as well as directives, and therefore in Hancher's terms they are 'commissive directives', since they commit the speaker to a certain course of behaviour. Furthermore invitations and offers require two participants to act, the speaker as well as the recipient, if they are to be accomplished successfully. Commissive directives "all look towards completion in some response by the hearer. (Hancher 1979:7). Commissive directives differ from simple directives which look for a recipient's response as the perlocutionary effect, in that the response looked for is illocutionary in character itself, and it can lead to a special complex illocutionary situation, i.e. to a 'cooperative illocutionary act'. The acceptance of, e.g. an offer or an invitation is a declaration. 'Unilateral illocutionary acts' such as invitations, offers and such, all look for an illocutionary act by the recipient, which is the response to the initial act. The effect of this is the 'cooperative illocutionary act', in which more than one person is involved. In providing this view on (certain types of) speech acts, Hancher makes an important step from a speaker-based speech act theory to a more interactional perspective on speech acts, in which both speaker and recipient get a place.

A similar perspective is to be found in Van Eemeren & Grootendorst (1982), who treat the illocutionary act of arguing when occurring in actual dialogue, as setting up the responsive illocutionary act of accepting the argumentation. Accepting the argumentation implies that the listener explicitly expresses that he accepts the argumentation, and why he does so.

As pointed out by several authors (e.g. Franck 1979; Levinson 1983), speech act theory has been criticized from the point of empirical studies of natural language use, among them CA and the ethnography of speaking. It has been shown by conversation analysts that the function which an utterance performs is largely due to its place within the conversation, or in a specific conversational sequence. For example, the utterance "Is Annet home?" can function as a request to call Annet to the telephone or to the door, or as a request for information, depending on its place within the conversation. In section 4.1 two rules of production and interpretation of this type of utterance are formulated in which the sequential position of the utterance plays a crucial part. The ethnography of speaking has drawn attention to the point that one and the same utterance may have different functions in different social settings. For example, an utterance such as "Why are you laughing?", a husband asking his wife, functions as a request for information; when a teacher addresses a pupil it will be understood by the pupil as 'Don't laugh'.

The function of utterances is thus conversationally dependent, which is one reason why CA prefers to speak of the 'conversational function' of an utterance (or series of utterances), rather than of its illocutionary force. And since CA studies utterances as they are being used in actual conversation, it is able to go beyond the concept of illocutionary force, and to see utterances as fulfilling specific functions. An utterance may function not only as a request, a question, or as invitation, it may also mark a change in topic, the starting or finishing of a story or the telling of a joke, acknowledging the previous information, or it may propose to close down the conversation. For example, the utterance "Okay, then we know enough for the time being," or "Sorry Ron, I'm going to brush my teeth, and I'll be going to bed", being produced in a telephone conversation, or even a single "O:kay", is recognizably taken up by the co-participant as a proposal to close down the conversation. Since speech act theory does not study speech acts in use, i.e. interactively (although it may make use of 'real' examples), it will be hard to see that language can do more than what the theoretician is able to think of while thinking about the function of language. As CA has convincingly shown there is a need for empirical and very detailed study of how people are using language.

Another problem for conversation analysts with speech act theory is the difference between types of speech acts is not always as clear as it seems. It is not always simple to decide how to label an utterance in speech acts terms (see e.g. Edmondson 1981; Franck 1984). The utterance "Could you call back in five minutes? She'll be there by then", said to the speaker who has asked to speak to caller's wife, may be labelled as a suggestion, a proposal, or a request. And in fact one can question the extent to which such differences are relevant for the participants themselves. Here it may suffice for the caller to know what to do if he wants to speak to her, i.e. call back five minutes later.

In this research I will speak of 'proposals' as a general category of conversational actions which all have in common that the recipient is asked to commit himself to the execution of an action: collaborating in bringing the present conversation to a close, passing on a piece of information to another person, calling somebody to the telephone, holding the line, accepting an offer, etc. All these actions have in common that they are initial or 'first' conversational actions to which the recipient is expected to respond. And although proposals may be rejected they are preferrably accepted or granted (see 3.4. on the preference organization of alternative responses).

1.2 The research data

The analysis to be presented is based on Dutch telephone conversations. With research into conversational interaction one can choose data which differ according to the criteria chosen, e.g. institutional versus everyday conversations, multi-party versus two-party conversations, and face-to-face versus telephone conversations. I will now discuss these types of differentiations.

1.2.1 Institutional versus everyday conversation

In CA research in general and in this study as well, the main goal is "the description and explication of the competences that ordinary speakers use and rely on in participating in intelligible, socially organized interaction.", as Heritage & Atkinson (1984:1) summarize it (see Chapter 2 for a more detailed discussion).

In general, conversations are studied where the organization is achieved by the participants themselves, and therefore, are not pre-structured. The length of the conversation, who speaks when and for how long and will say what, etc., is all organized by the participants themselves (cf. Sacks et al. 1974/1978). One reason for the primacy of everyday conversation as the analytic object of CA is the fact that this is the order of interaction to which a person is first exposed to the social world. Everyday conversation constitutes the communicative framework that a child must master the conventions of as a condition for being a competent member of society.

Although everyday conversations form the basic object of CA research, institutional interactions (doctor-patient, judicial, classroom interaction, etc.), are also studied. An important difference between everyday and institutional talk is that certain features of institutional interaction are pre-structured to a certain extent, depending on the type of institution. The social roles themselves are relatively fixed: doctor or patient, judge or defendant, teacher or pupil. These roles are related partly to certain rights and obligations, and partly to the tasks to be performed, which derive from the function of the interaction. Such institutional interactions may be oriented to an agenda (overt or not), and are pre-structured in several ways. The time of the interaction is limited or even set, the teacher does the teaching, the judge does the questioning, and the pupils and the defendants do what they are supposed to do. It is up to the judge or the teacher to decide when the interaction will be closed. It is up to the patient to recount the symptoms, and up to the doctor to carry out the examination and treatment. Although this does not imply that the participants are only playing their prescribed roles, they are to a certain extent restricted by these roles.

In everyday conversation there are not such clear cut rights, obligations, and tasks, but this does not mean that they do not exist at all. There may well be rights and obligations related to another level of an interpersonal relationship, such as differences in age, social status, sex, or expertise regarding the topic under discussion. The consequences of these differences in conversation are less fixed, and therefore more negotiable. Everyday conversations then, are less determined by factors outside the conversation itself, and are therefore more amenable to analysis of general conversational procedures than institutional interactions are.

1.2.2 Two-party versus multi-party conversation

The second difference exists between two-party and multi-party conversations. In two-party conversations there are a speaker and a recipient, and these conversational roles alternate constantly. By virtue of the absence of other participants the recipient is always the addressee of the speaker's talk, and will always be the next speaker when the turn alternates.

In the case of multi-party conversations however, a speaker can address to a certain extent, just one of the co-participants. Non-speaking participants may therefore differ as to the roles they have during this type of conversation or during parts of it. They may be addressees or just listeners.

Since the research to be presented is based on two-party conversations, there are only two participants: the speaker and the recipient. Only in some cases a third party is involved, for example, when someone on the telephone is talking to someone else in the room.

1.2.3 Face-to-face versus telephone conversation

In the case of face-to-face conversations the participants share a physical space, and everything occurs in that space. The participants themselves are also part of this space and therefore they are visible to one another, which has consequences for the conversation. First of all they can talk about and refer to objects and happenings located in the shared physical space. This enables them to use deictic expressions such as 'Look over there', or 'Gosh, that's beautiful', or 'What a nice hat you've got'.

The participants of a telephone conversation however, do not share the same visible world, and therefore they simply cannot refer to objects and events invisible for the co-participant. In order to make the co-participant understand, such referring is necessarily done explicitly, for example:

(1) [HH:TC:18:104]
V. Hold on. I'll turn the TV set down, because I can hardly hear you. (Are watching a football game, y'know.)

Also the speaker may indicate that the next utterance will be addressed to someone else invisible for the co-participant:

(2) [HH:TC:18:35:65]
V. One moment Reina. Hello boy. There's a child of mine coming in.

As these fragments show, when telephone conversationalists refer to events occurring in their own physical space, they do so explicitly, or when they talk to somebody else in the room, they make this clear. This makes these facts accessible not only to the co-participant, but to the analyst as well.

Conversationalists may also refer to the physical actions they are performing during the conversation. This happens in the next fragment of a telephone conversation when speaker R, who has recently had her leg operated upon, is going to sit down:

(3) [HH:TC:18:60]
V. How are you,
R. Well fine.
V. Are you?
→ R. Let me sit down. Oops-a-daisy. Okay.

In telephone conversations the participants are not in the position of seeing their co-participants performing physical actions, which means that when speakers want to refer to these actions, they have to be described rather than being deictically referred to. Such 'action-describing talk' is often found in telephone conversations such as when a telephone number is being taken down: "I'll write it down. One, nine, fou:r (.) four five six". In face-to-face conversations on the other hand we may find 'action-accompanying talk'. Action-accompanying talk and action-describing talk may be differentiated from 'conversational talk' which only has a function within and for the conversation as such, and which constitutes the conversation.

Whereas face-to-face interaction may show a relatively high proportion of action-accompanying talk, telephone conversations in principle consist of conversational talk only. And as far as objects and events being discussed are invisible for the co-participant, this will be recognizable as such for the co-participant (as well as for the analyst of the conversation).

The shared world of telephone conversationalists is the conversation itself, and every utterance has its meaning and function in being part of this complex activity. On these grounds then, a silence occurring in the conversation is to be treated as a conversational action having a meaning for the conversation.

In case of face-to-face conversation however, a silence may mean that there is temporarily no conversation and no interaction because the former conversationalists are perhaps now watching television or reading a paper. Face-to-face conversations do not have a marked beginning and ending in the way telephone conversations have, and the first can be postponed and taken up again without being marked as such, as long as two or more people are in the same place together.

This explains why silences in telephone conversations are filled with verbal elements such as "uh" or "well uh", whereas in face-to-face conversations silences may be filled by actions other than speaking.

We may summarize by saying that telephone conversations are continuous verbal activities, and insofar as actions are being discussed, this will be marked as such in one way or another. Face-to-face conversations by contrast, may be social actions which are embedded in, or alternate with, other actions. The linguistic activities may be, but need not be, conversational activities. They may also accompany physical activities or comment on events happening in the shared visible world. It is clear that the distinction between conversational talk and action-accompanying talk will not always be evident. That is, one may refer to what one is doing, but one can also use this action as a topic for conversation.

This diffuseness of the function of verbal actions constitutes a methodological problem for the analysis of face-to-face conversation, together with the fact that the participants make use of non-verbal actions in addition to verbal ones. As Ch. Goodwin (1981) and M. Goodwin (1980) have convincingly shown, there is an interrelationship between the use of verbal and nonverbal conversational activities. An analysis of face-to-face conversation can therefore only be adequate when nonverbal activities are taken into consideration, which means that these conversations should be video-recorded.

However, video-recording of naturally occurring conversation faces its own methodological problems. Since CA especially sees everyday life (including institutional life), as its analytic object, it is crucially important that the data to be analyzed are natural. Video-recording these conversations however, may easily affect the natural behaviour.

Telephone conversations compared with other conversations have the following advantages:

- The data are reduced to conversations of a solely verbal character, to which the analyst has as much access as the participants.
- All the activities are in principle conversational activities. When they are not, this will be indicated by the conversationalists, and will therefore also be accessible to the analyst.
- A telephone conversation is a continuous activity. When it is interrupted, it will be indicated by the conversationalists themselves.
- Telephone conversations in general are two-party conversations with a speaker and a recipient, the latter also being the addressee and the next speaker.

For all the above reasons, telephone conversations may be seen as the most compact form of conversation, i.e. with the strongest focus on the verbal means, and with a maximum of access for the analyst, which makes them ideal for analysis of verbal conversational devices.

My analysis is therefore based on telephone conversations for they contain the most restricted type of data, at the same time being both natural and unsimplified.

1.3 Recording, transcription and translation of the data

In this section attention will be paid to the recordings and transcription of the data, as well as how these transcriptions have been translated into English, and the problems one is confronted with when one wishes to publish Dutch conversational data in English.

1.3.1 Recording

The data on which the analysis is based derive from around eight hours of Dutch conversation by telephone, recorded by friends and acquaintances of the author. In the non-analytical chapters, Anglo-American conversational data provided by Gail Jefferson or published elsewhere, have sometimes been used. Most of the Dutch conversations have been recorded at home, and concern topics that people usually talk about on the telephone. In some cases the recording is broken off before the actual end of the conversation, perhaps because the topic to be discussed was not considered to be a 'public' one. A minority of the conversations have been recorded at work, and these are usually on business topics.

The people who recorded the conversations were told only that the purpose of the recordings was to investigate "how people take their turns in conversation, and that sort of thing". As they did not have any special knowledge of CA, there is no reason to assume that these conversations would differ from unrecorded ones with respect to the phenomena to be analyzed. On theoretical grounds it might be assumed that the conversationalists may possibly have used a more formal speech style than they would otherwise have done, especially at the start of their recording-activity (cf. Labov 1972b), but - as far as this may indeed be the case - since speech-style is not part of this research, it is not considered a problem here.

1.3.2 Transcription

CA attention to fine details of conversation requires a detailed transcription of the data. This does not imply a claim that the transcript captures all the possible details of the recordings.

The transcription system used here has been developed

by Gail Jefferson. The transcription key is to be found in the Appendix.

Some of the tape recordings have been initially transcribed by Rob Rombouts and Judith de Venster, to whom I wish to express my gratitude here.

1.3.3 Translation

Since the analysis to be presented here is based on Dutch conversations, the data have been translated into English (the original Dutch fragments are to be found in the Appendix). The translations have been checked and corrected by my colleagues in the language department, mostly by Pieter Nieuwint.

The data have been translated in such a way that two criteria have been met, the first being that the sense of the original text should become clear, and the second that the translation should keep as close as possible to the Dutch text. These two criteria are difficult to meet at the same time if one wants to present an English translation which looks like colloquial English conversation. On several occasions it was decided to choose a relatively poor translation in order to retain certain characteristics of the Dutch conversations essential for the analysis.

One possible way to present the data would have been to provide two translations. A literal word-for-word translation might have been added; however, even if one would give a word-for-word translation of certain parts of a Dutch sentence, the result would often be incomprehensible. Due partly to the pragmatic specifics of different languages the literal translation of a certain sentence has a meaning different from that in the source language. Word-for-word translation therefore is a quasi-scientific solution to a problem which can hardly, if at all, be solved.

English and Dutch differ from one another in syntactic as well as semantic-pragmatic aspects. With respect to semantic-pragmatic differences it should be pointed out that whereas Dutch expresses expressive functions of language mainly by means of modal particles ("hoor", "wel", "maar", "toch", "even", and combinations of these), in English this task is mainly performed by intonation patterns on the one hand (cf. Schubiger 1965), and as far as I can see, by a refined system of verb-use and verbal inflection on the other.

Another problem concerns ambiguous words or phrases in the Dutch data, especially when the ambiguity in question plays some role in the conversation. In such cases the translation may cause problems. This happens especially when a further difference between Dutch and English comes into the picture, i.e. when two seemingly equivalent words turn out to differ in their emotional or connotational load, as is often the case.

An attempt has been made as best as feasable to solve such problems of translation by annotating the translated data, or by providing two English alternatives.

It will be clear that, whereas the Dutch data as provided in this study, are transcriptions of the recorded conversations, the English translations are not translations of the Dutch transcribed conversations, but translations of the analyzed and interpreted conversations.

Despite all the problems of translating conversations, it is nevertheless important to publish non-English data-analyses in English, since English is the main language for scientific publication. If CA is to describe general conversational features and procedures it needs publications based on studies of other languages, but made available in a language such as English.

2 Ethnomethodological conversation analysis: Some general principles

The methodological approach of the research presented here is that of Conversation Analysis. Chapter 2 will briefly point out some notions important for the understanding of CA. I will first say something about ethnomethodology, being the mother discipline of CA, and then will point out some of the general theoretical and methodological standpoints of CA itself. In the next chapter, some of these points will be discussed in more detail.

2.1 Ethnomethodology

In the 1960's a group of sociologists, calling themselves ethnomethodologists, broke out of the traditional sociological theoretical framework. The main founder of the group was Harold Garfinkel.

The general interest of Ethnomethodology is formed by the methods, the rules people use in order to make sense of other peoples' behaviour, and to render their own behaviour understandable to others. Rather than seeing rules as guidances for social action, rules are seen as being used to decide the meaning of what was done in a certain situation, and in that sense as constitutive for social action.

Garfinkel uses the term ethnomethodology to refer to "the investigation of the rational properties of indexical expressions and other practical actions as contingent ongoing accomplishments of organized artful practices of everyday life." (Garfinkel 1967b:11). Greatbatch refers to ethnomethodology as "the study of the competences which underlie socially organized interaction." (Greatbatch 1985:87-88). The facts of social reality are not seen as fixed facts, as in traditional sociology, but as the results of human action (including linguistic action), and interaction, i.e. as 'social accomplishments'. A recurrent theme in the ethnomethodological literature therefore, is to 'treat facts as accomplishments'.

The strictly ethnomethodological view on social reality has been critized. For example, T. Wilson (1985) declares that social interaction and social structure are reflexively related in such a way that social structure is simultaneously a resource for, and reproduced through, social interaction. (cf. Maynard & Wilson 1980, Wilson & Zimmerman 1981; see also Atkinson & Drew 1979 and Schegloff (fc)).

A crucial notion in the ethnomethodological tradition is that of 'member'. Garfinkel & Sacks say that they "do not use the term to refer to a person. It refers instead to mastery of natural language, which we understand in the following way. We offer the observation that persons, because of the fact that they are heard to be speaking a natural language, SOMEHOW are heard to be engaged in the objective production and objective display of commonsense knowledge of everyday activities as observable and reportable phenomena." (Garfinkel & Sacks 1970:342). Unlike Garfinkel and Sacks, I prefer to use the term member to refer to whoever masters natural language in the sense Garfinkel & Sacks circumscribe this. The notion of 'member' is close to the sociolinguistic notion of 'communicative competence' introduced by Hymes (1971), and extended by Gumperz as "the knowledge of linguistic and related communicative conventions that speakers must have to initiate and sustain conversational involvement." (Gumperz 1982:325).

Ethnomethodology sees interaction as an interpretive process, or more precisely, as a process of 'documentary interpretation' (Garfinkel 1962). An actor perceives the behaviour of his co-participant as a meaningful action. On the basis of what the co-participant is presumed to mean, the actor decides how to deal with this action. In this sense social action is intrinsically interactional in character. It is also an interpretive action since actions are based on the actor's interpretations of the co-participant's actions. This implies that interpretations are not made once and for all; depending on what will happen next, an action may be reinterpreted. An utterance may be initially heard as a joke, whereas it may be reinterpreted later on as a serious remark. Apart from this, meanings may develop and change in the course of the interaction. What initially has been heard - and perhaps been meant - as a teasing, may gradually and in retrospect change into an offensive remark (cf. T.Wilson 1971:66-70).

Social actors, e.g. conversationalists, demonstrate the interpretations they have made of the actions of their co-participants by their responses to these actions. By saying "Yeah, let's go home" in response to "It's twelve o'clock", a recipient shows that he has understood the prior utterance as a suggestion to go home. On the other hand the recipient may understand the prior utterance as just a remark, or he may act as if he does not understand the suggestive character of the utterance by saying "So what?". For an analyst it remains unclear whether or not the hearer has indeed interpreted the utterance in the way the response seems to indicate. For this reason CA prefers to speak of the co-participant's 'treatment' of an action, rather than of its interpretation. In responding to the utterance "Haven't you done the dishes?", with a "No", the recipient treats the prior utterance as a Yes/No question; in responding to it with a "No, why don't you do it?", the prior utterance is treated as a complaint. The way in which a hearer responds to an action, i.e. treats an action, thus provides a proof-procedure for the understanding of the action's meaning. And when the initial speaker sees that his utterance has been understood incorrectly, he may become more explicit in what he actually has meant by his utterance. Initial speaker may do a 'third turn repair' (Schegloff 1979), that is, he may produce a turn after the response (where the recipient's understanding is revealed), in which a repair of that response is done (cf. Heritage 1984a).

An action receives its meaning, among other things, by virtue of the context in which it is produced; phrased differently, meanings are 'indexical'. This notion is from Bar-Hillel (1954) who introduced the term 'indexical expression', for what in linguistics is more usually called a 'deictic expression' ("this", "there", "she", "her", etc. See Lyons 1977, Chapter 15). Garfinkel uses the more general term of 'indexical particular' which is not restricted to purely linguistic events. The indexical property of talk lies in the fact that people usually do not state explicitly the intended meaning of their utterances, and that the context from which an utterance draws, is part of what guides the linguistic form, and the understanding of an utterance. In terms of speech act theory speakers usually do not explicitly provide the illocutionary force of their utterances. They greet by saying "Hello", without explaining that they intend to greet when they are saying "Hello".

The 'documentary interpretation' of actions, according to Wilson, consists of: "identifying an underlying pattern behind a series of appearances such that each appearance is seen as referring to, an expression of, or a "document of", the underlying pattern. However, the underlying pattern itself is identified through its individual concrete appearances, so that the appearances reflecting the pattern and the pattern itself mutually determine one another in the same way that the "part" and the "whole" mutually determine each other in gestalt phenomena. This mutual determination of appearances and underlying pattern is referred to by Garfinkel as indexicality, and a particular appearance is called an indexical particular. A central characteristic of documentary interpretation is that later appearances may force a revision in the perceived underlying pattern that in turn compels a reinterpretation of what previous appearances "really were". Moreover, on any given occasion present appearances are interpreted partially on the basis of what the underlying pattern projects as the future course of events, and one may have to await further developments to understand the meaning of present appearances. In this sense, documentary interpretations are retrospective and prospective." (Wilson 1971:68).

Expressions are often vague and equivocal and may have several meanings when no context has been supplied. This 'context' consists of ethnographical particulars of the speaker, the relationship between speaker and hearer, the setting in which an action is produced (i.e. the 'social context'), including what has been said so far (i.e. the 'sequential' or 'conversational context'). The context is not stable and fixed. The contextual particulars that make up the context are assembled by the hearer to decide the specific sense of the talk, and anything can be used as a part of the contextual particular.

The elements of the context are continually shifting, and they can therefore change the meaning of the action. The context itself is partially made up of indexical expressions, and a hearer has to make sense of the context as well. So not only utterances may be ambiguous, but contexts may as well. Since actions receive their meaning within the context, their sense is 'context-sensitive'. But since they also form part of, and add to the context, actions are 'context-renewing'.

This view on interaction as a process of documentary interpretation has as its methodological implication that "the study of interaction would have to be made from the position of the actor. Since action is forged by the actor out of what he perceives, interprets, and judges, one would have to see the operating situation as the actor sees it, perceive objects as the actor perceives them, ascertain their meaning in terms of the meaning they have for the actor, and follow the actor's line of conduct as the actor organizes it - in short, one would have to take the role of the actor and see the world from his standpoint." (Blumer 1966:542, cited in Wilson 1971:69). In order to be able to describe an action the analyst must engage in documentary interpretation. This means that the analyst's descriptions are themselves documentary interpretations, and are therefore 'interpretive descriptions'.

The context-sensitivity of the interpretation of actions and utterances accounts for the fact that CA does not investigate utterances isolated from their conversational contexts. In CA literature one usually will find rather long fragments of conversation where the instance-to-be-described occurs. In giving such larger fragments the analyst provides the context which he thinks has been the relevant one for the conversationalists, which means that this particular fragment is the analyst's interpretation of the conversationalists' interpretation of what has been relevant for their interpretation of the utterance in question.

Conversation analysts therefore, seem to be making 'second order interpretations'. There is no objective way for deciding which information conversationalists may have been using in their understanding of an utterance and making themselves understandable. The most an analyst can do is to be as explicit as possible, and show the reader how he has come to the analysis being presented. This 'weakness' of making second order interpretations however, holds only to a certain extent, since CA is mainly trying to locate, and account for patterns - particularly sequential ones - in conversation. These patterns have a certain objectivity, as they are the results of regularities in actors' interpretations.

For a more detailed description of these ethnomethodological notions I refer to the work of Garfinkel (1967a), Garfinkel & Sacks (1970), Mehan & Wood (1975), Heritage (1984a), Leiter (1980), and the reader by Douglas (1971).

2.2 Ethnomethodological Conversation Analysis

Within this field of research the specific orientation to everyday conversation as a research object has been initiated by Harvey Sacks. Due to his early death Sacks' work consists mainly of unpublished lecture notes, which have been partly transcribed, edited, and published by his earliest students and colleagues, one of them Gail

Jefferson. Sacks' work has been, and is continued by Gail Jefferson, Emanuel Schegloff, and others. Most of their work is based directly on Sacks' observations these scholars have analyzed systematically, and in greater detail.

CA has been taken up by linguists who have come to realize that conversation is the context in which spoken language is produced. This shift in perspective on language use may be best illustrated by Gumperz (1982), who begins his article "The linguistic bases of communicative competence" by referring to a session at the Georgetown University Round Table on Languages and Linguistics in 1972, where Sacks delivered a paper on punning. Gumperz remembers that "the room was only partly filled and, in fact, several listeners walked out muttering that they could not understand the speaker" who "introduced basic theoretical notions by means of descriptive phrases such as: 'sequential ordering', 'positioning of utterances', 'the interactional job that utterances do'." (Gumperz 1982:323).

The CA perspective on spoken language has made sociolinguists and pragmaticians pay more attention to the role of conversational interaction, when they study, for example, first and second language acquisition, or what people do with language. And it may be expected that the bridge between sociological CA and linguistic pragmatics will become stronger in the near future.

The basic goal of CA research is, as Heritage & Atkinson put it "the description and explication of the competences that ordinary speakers use and rely on in participating in intelligible, socially organized interaction. At its most basic, this objective is one of describing the procedures by which conversationalists produce their own behavior and understand and deal with the behavior of others. A basic assumption throughout is Garfinkel's (1967b:1) proposal that these activities - producing conduct and understanding and dealing with it - are accomplished as the accountable products of common sets of procedures." (Heritage & Atkinson 1984:1).

The analysis of large collections of everyday conversations exhibits order. As Schegloff & Sacks (1973) have pointed out, conversations turn out to be orderly because they are methodically produced by the participants for one another. The objective of the analysis, then, is to describe and explicate the ways in which co-participants produce such orderly organized conversations. For example, if one studies collections of conversations between different people, with varying kinds of relationships and backgrounds, it turns out that these conversations overwhelmingly exhibit the same ways in which they are opened and closed, topics are developed and changed, stories and jokes are initiated, told and terminated, compliments and invitations are accepted or rejected, etc.

The methods used by conversationalists can be subjected to formal analytical description. Citing Sacks when he sums up some of the central findings of his work: "The detailed ways in which actual, naturally occurring social activities occur are subjectable to formal description. Social activities - actual, singular sequences of them - are methodical occurrences. That is, their description consists of the description of sets of formal procedures persons employ. The methods persons employ to produce their activities permit formal description of singular occurrences that are generalizable in intuitively nonapparent ways and are highly reproducibly usable." (Sacks 1984a:21). Such a formal description of formal procedures used by conversationalists can be found in Sacks et al. 1974/1978, where they describe how conversationalists allocate speaking turns in a structured way, and how this 'turn-taking machinery' consists of a set of methods by which the successive contributions result in an orderly social organization, a conversation. (See Chapter 3 for further details of turn-taking).

Stating that conversationalists have a set of methods at hand which they apply for solving conversational problems, does not mean that conversing is a mechanic and determined business. As Jefferson says, a conversation is not determined by structural provisions only, but also by what conversationalists do with them. This "suggests that there is a distinction between structural provisions and participants' work, where a given segment of talk is the result of the cooperation of those two; that is, is the result of participants' work in carrying out structural provisions." (Jefferson 1972:315).

Conversation analysts show not only that conversations are orderly as such, but also show that this order is the product of the co-participants' methodical actions, and by which methods this orderliness has been achieved. Furthermore they try to demonstrate that conversationalists are 'normatively oriented' to such regularities. This normative orientation of conversationalists to the regularity of conversational practices becomes especially clear from the analysis of what may look like deviant cases or counter-examples. For example, the fact that a question may not be answered at times does not mean that such instances are counter examples to the rule that conversationalists are normatively oriented to questions receiving answers. Instead CA will use such instances to show that the answers are 'noticeably absent' (Sacks Nov.15, 1971, Ch.2:23), which may become clear when the questioner repeats his question.

The objective of CA is the analysis of conversationalists' shared methods, rather than the analysis of their differences and the conditions under which conversationalists may proceed differently. It is considered important to gain maximum understanding of the shared methods before starting to divide them into smaller subcategories [1], and to study the conditions under which one or another subtype is applied.

Speech act theory (Austin 1962, Searle 1969) has forwarded the view in linguistics that in producing utterances, speakers accomplish actions, e.g. questions, requests, promises, invitations, etc. This theory gives analytic primacy to isolated utterances, and accounts for variations in the uptake of the utterances according to the conditions in which they are uttered. This kind of analysis has been criticized by authors like Streeck (1980) and Levinson (1981), who point out that utterances are understood by reference to their placement within a sequence of actions. For this reason the primary units of CA research are sequences, and turns within sequences.

Turns project in a relatively strong way a relevant next action or a range of actions, to be produced by another speaker in the next turn. This phenomenon is referred to as the 'sequential implicativeness' of a turn of talk (Schegloff & Sacks 1973). Strong instances of this phenomenon are 'adjacency pairs', such as the question-answer pair, the greeting-greeting pair, and the like, of which the 'first pair-part' projects a relevant 'second pair-part'. Heritage & Atkinson say that: "Once it is recognized that some current or "first" action projects some appropriate "second", it becomes relevant to examine the various ways in which a second speaker may accomplish such a second, or analyzably withhold its accomplishment, or avoid its accomplishment by undertaking some other activity. If it can then be shown that the producers of the first action deal in systematically organized ways with a variety of alternative seconds (or a noticeably absent second), then it will also be demonstrated that the object of investigation is an institutionalized organization for the activity in question that is systematically oriented to by speakers.

These observations can be generalized outward from the comparatively simple adjacency-pair organization by remarking that virtually every utterance (...) occurs at some structurally defined place in talk (...). Thus the vast majority of utterances occur as selections from a field of possibilities made relevant by some prior utterance, and in their turn project a range of possible "nexts". Most utterances, therefore, can be analyzed as dealing with a prior in some way and, among other things, as indicating their producers' preparedness to forward, acquiesce in, or resist the course of action aimed at by an earlier speaker. (...) No empirically occurring utterance ever occurs outside, or external to, some specific sequence. Whatever is said will be said in some sequential context, and its illocutionary force will be determined by reference to what it accomplishes in relation to some sequentially prior utterance or set of utterances." (Heritage & Atkinson 1984:6).

The authors are right in using the hedging "most" in their remark that "Most utterances, therefore, can be analyzed as dealing with a prior in some way", since not all utterances can be analyzed in relation to a prior, and therefore the sequential placement of an utterance is not the only basis for its actional status. Especially sequence-initial utterances (e.g. questions) are usually not analyzable by reference to their sequential placement (cf. Goffman 1976:51). Although there is clearly no one-to-one relationship between linguistic form and actional function (cf. Schegloff 1980), linguistic aspects may co-establish the interpretation of utterances. For example, an utterance may contain a preverbal 'please' ("Can you please pass the salt?"), 'would' or 'could' ("Could you pass the salt?"), which makes the utterances interpretable as requests.

It may be said that CA tends to pay too little attention to the linguistic and text-linguistic features of utterances, when they take such a sequential standpoint. Reference may be made here to Brown & Yule (1983) for an interesting attempt to treat 'Discourse Analysis' as a synthesis of several linguistic, sociological, psychological and computational approaches.

Furthermore aspects of the social setting in which social interaction takes place tend to be neglected by CA, as Levinson (1979) and T. Wilson (1985) point out. Levinson makes use of the concept of speech event as it was introduced in the Ethnography of Speaking approach. A speech event is a culturally recognized social activity (e.g. teaching), in which language plays a specific role. Given that such cultural events constrain the use of language, corresponding inference rules seem to operate assigning functions to utterances partly on the basis of the social situation within which the talk is conducted. Thus when a school-teacher says "Why are you laughing?" it will be heard as a command to stop laughing rather than as a request for information, by virtue of the institutional setting in which it occurs.

This type of reasoning is also found in the work of Wilson. In a paper on the relation between social structure (by which he refers to both relational and institutional components) and social interaction, Wilson (1985) notes that not only the sequential context of a particular utterance is important, but also the relational and institutional context. In order to illustrate this point he discusses the utterance in the second line of the following fragment of an emergency call to the police:

(4) [Wilson 1985, simplified]
D. Midcity emergensee:
→ C. .hh um: yeah (.) somebody jus' vandalized my car,
D. .hh what's your address
C. (forty:) oh seven Grantwood ((background voices))
D. is this a house or an apartment
C. ih: tst a hou:se
D. uh your las' name.
C. (Geer)
D. How you spell it
C. gee ar ee ee ar:
D. We'll sen' someone out to see you.
C. Than' you.=
D. =umhum bye.
C. By-

Wilson poses the question why the utterance "somebody jus' vandalized my=car" is heard as a request when the lexical or grammatical features of this utterance give no indication for this interpretation. For his analysis of this fragment he uses the notions of 'membership categorization device' (MCD) and 'category-bound activity' [2] (Sacks 1972a, 1972b).

In the first turn of the fragment the answerer of the call identifies herself with the 'categorical identity' of a complaint taker "Midcity emergensee:". There are activities bound to the categories of a complaint maker and a complaint taker, notably, making complaints and supplying relevant information on the one hand, and taking complaints, assessing them, and sending assistance where warranted, on the other. The utterance "somebody jus' vandalized my car" is heard under the auspices of a hearer's maxim to regard it as an action bound to the category of caller to an emergency dispatching service, that is, as a request for help.

In fact CA research does deal with the social setting of conversation, but it tends to take these aspects for granted since it gives primacy to a sequential approach of the analysis of utterances. But one should be aware not to see sequential placement as the only or the most important factor of interpretation of utterances.

Wilson (1985) points out that the idea of social context has a place in CA through the notion of recipient design. By 'recipient design' (Sacks F'1971, L4 & L5) is meant that a given utterance is directed to, and built for this particular recipient in this particular interaction. Relevant aspects of the participants' relationship are their shared biographies, their institutional identities, and the institutional setting of the interaction.

Since CA studies the regularity and the methodically established orderliness of utterances it will be clear that it uses collections of conversational data rather than single conversations. It is only in the analysis of larger collections of data that the shared methods of conversationalists may become apparent. "Our aim is to get into a position to transform, in an almost literal, physical sense, our view of "what happened", from a matter of a particular interaction done by particular people, to a matter of interactions as products of a machinery. We are trying to find the machinery." (Sacks 1984a:26-27).

This methodical choice for collecting instances also accounts for the tendency to pay attention to the features of the linguistic form and the setting as explaining factors only when this is really necessary. In principle the data concern naturally occurring conversations organized by the participants themselves. All the aspects of the conversation, i.e. the topic, how a topic will be initiated and terminated, and by whom, who will say what and when and how, how speaking turns are allocated, how the conversation is closed off, are problems solved by the participants, using the methods they have for solving these problems (Sacks et al. 1974/ 1978).

3 The sequential organization of conversation

3.1 Conversational turn-taking

In this chapter I will discuss the most prominent interest of CA research, i.e. the sequential organization of speech activities in conversation. In his unpublished Lecture Notes one can see how Sacks developed his ideas on how conversation is organized turn-by-turn, and how these successively produced turns are rlated to each other. A turn is related to its prior turn, as well as to the next one, resulting in conversationalists produce inter-related strings of turns. When such a series of turns have a special inter-relationship they constitute a sequence.

Sequential organization also holds for larger parts of the conversation; the opening and closing section of conversations, jokes, and stories are all organized by the conversationalists in their own ways.

An important moment for CA was the publication of Sacks, Schegloff & Jefferson's article on the management of conversational turn-taking in 1974 (which interestingly enough appeared in the linguistic journal "Language"). It was republished in a slightly revised version by Schenkein in 1978. This second publication will be referred to in the discussion of the turn-taking model hereafter.

Sacks et al. propose the existence of some formal apparatus for turn-taking for conversation which is context-free in the sense that it can be used for the organization of any type of verbal interaction. To be able to describe such an apparatus, they studied tape recordings of naturally occurring conversations from which they derived the following characteristics:

1. "Speaker change recurs, or, at least, occurs.
2. Overwhelmingly, one party talks at a time.
3. Occurrences of more than one speaker at a time are common, but brief.
4. Transitions from one turn to a next with no gap

and no overlap between them are common. Together with transitions characterized by slight gap or slight overlap, they make up the vast majority of transitions.
5. Turn order is not fixed, but varies.
6. Turn size is not fixed, but varies.
7. Length of conversation is not fixed, specified in advance.
8. What parties say is not fixed, specified in advance.
9. Relative distribution of turns is not fixed, specified in advance.
10. Number of parties can change.
11. Turn-allocation techniques are obviously used. A current speaker may select a next speaker (as when a current speaker addresses a question to another party); parties may self-select, in starting to talk.
12. Various "turn-constructional units" are employed. Turns can be projectedly "one word long", or, for example, they can be sentential in length.
13. Repair mechanisms for dealing with turn-taking errors and violations obviously are available for use. For example, if two parties find themselves talking at the same time, one of them will stop prematurely, thus repairing the trouble."

(Sacks et al. 1978:10-11)

These conversational facts are accounted for by a model for turn-taking. Sacks et al. describe their model in terms of two components, the 'turn-constructional component' and the 'turn-allocation component'.

Then a set of rules governs turn-construction providing for the allocation of a turn to a next conversational party. The rules also provide for a turn transfer which minimizes gap and overlap.

With respect to the turn-constructional component Sacks et al. point out that there are various unit-types for turn-construction: lexical, phrasal, clausal, and sentential constructions. Instances of the unit-types allow a projection of the unit-type-in-progress. This projection-capacity of unit-types enables participants to know which syntactic components it will take for the unit-type to be completed. A speaker employing a certain unit-type is entitled to complete this unit. The first possible completion of this unit constitutes an initial transition-relevance place. Turn-taking is co-ordinated by reference to such places (I will come back to this later).

There are two groups of turn-allocational techniques:

the current speaker selecting the next speaker, and the next speaker self-selecting. Turn-taking is governed by a set of hierarchically ordered rules. Sacks et al. say that "For any turn:

1. At initial turn-constructional unit's initial transition-relevance place:
(a) If the turn-so-far is so constructed as to involve the use of a "current speaker selects next" technique, then the party so selected has rights, and is obliged, to take a next turn to speak, and no others have such rights or obligations, transfer occurring at that place.
(b) If the turn-so-far is so constructed as not to involve the use of a "current speaker selects next" technique, self-selection for next speakership may, but need not, be instituted, with first starter acquiring rights to a turn, transfer occurring at that place.
(c) If the turn-so-far is so constructed as not to involve the use of a "current speaker selects next" technique, then current speaker may, but need not, continue, unless another self-selects.
2. If, at initial turn-constructional unit's initial transition-relevance place, neither 1(a) nor 1(b) has operated, and, following the provision of 1(c), current speaker has continued, then the Rule-set (a)-(c) re-applies at next transition-relevance place, and recursively at each next transition-relevance place, until transfer is effected."
(op.cit.:12-13)

For a more detailed explanation of this turn-taking model the reader is referred to the article itself, or to Chapter 2 of Atkinson & Drew, 1979. Only a few aspects of the model will be discussed in further detail here.

This turn-taking system accounts for the conversational facts listed above. I will give one example here. The fact that, overwhelmingly, one party talks at a time is accounted for by rule 1(a). In spite of the fact that conversationalists are oriented to this 'one-speaker-at-a-time rule' overlaps do frequently occur. As Jefferson showed on several occasions (Jefferson 1973, 1983a) a turn-constructional unit may project which lexical items are coming up. This projection-capacity of turn-constructional units enables the next speaker to start up his next turn shortly before the completion of the current turn. For example,

(5) [SBL:10:12, from Schegloff 1972:107]
B. why don't you come and see
me some[times.
→ A. [I would like to

There are two problems with respect to this turn-taking model. One concerns the syntactical definition of the units of the turn-constructional component. The other concerns the hierarchical ordering of the rules for turn-taking (this will be discussed in section 3.2).

Turns are said to be constructed of instances of unit-types which are syntactically defined: lexical, phrasal, clausal, and sentential constructions. The first possible completion of such a unit constitutes an initial transition-relevance place.

The main problem however is that syntactic components, other and smaller than sentences, may coincide with a complete turn or utterance [1].

As already pointed out by Sacks et al., a turn may consist of a single word, for example in case of Wh-questions ("What?"), or a single phrase ("In Spain"), as an answer to a question like "Where did you hear that?". Especially since such elliptical constructions are often found in conversation, defining turn-constructional units purely syntactically is inadequate.

When discussing turn-taking in his Lecture Notes of Nov.15, 1971, and elsewhere, Sacks refers to 'complete utterances' as well as to 'sentence completion', after which speaker-change may occur. He looks upon sentences as a general structuring device for utterances which go through a process of incompletion, upcomingness of completion, and accomplishing completion. This completion process of utterances plays an important role in the next speaker selection techniques. Syntactically speaking a clause or a phrase should be seen as an incomplete sentence. On pragmatic-linguistic (i.e. textlinguistic) and conversation-analytical grounds however, such a syntactic component may very well be a complete conversational utterance.

Using syntactic notions for describing utterance- or turn-completion thus may cause problems. It may be said that although conversationalists use syntactic structures this does not imply that a complete utterance matches per se a well-formed sentence. Sentences are ideal syntactic structures formed accordingly to language-specific rules. Conversationalists however, seem to apply linguistic rules only to a certain extent. Utterances may be ill-formed in many respects (syntactically, morphologically, phonologically, or semantically), yet the conversationalists may treat them as 'adequate complete utterances' (cf. Sacks F'1966, L9:9-11) [2].

Conversationalists are not to be seen as people who construct sentences i.e. utterances; their main concern is to produce conversational actions (e.g. asking questions and answering them), and they do so by means of utterances. And since the current recipient is supposed to respond to his co-participant's actions his primary task is to analyze the current utterance for its sequential impact: what is the recipient supposed to do next, and when should this be done? When this is clear to the recipient the current utterance is in principle complete enough to be taken over (Schegloff (1980:150) speaks of 'completed-for-response-utterances'), and mainly because of the rule of 'one-at-a-time' a current speaker may finish his utterance-in-progress. This phenomenon of utterances being complete enough is also the basis for overlap, whereas it is partly by virtue of its linguistic structure that an utterance projects what has not yet been said.

3.2 Turns and Discourse Units

The second problematic point of the turn-taking model concerns the fact that when turn-transition occurs on sentence-completion points, this means that if a speaker reaches such a completion point while not having selected a next speaker, another party may self-select. However, an empirical fact of naturally occurring conversation (though not mentioned in the list of Sacks et al.), is that conversationalists make turns larger than just one sentence. They tell jokes and stories, or they develop arguments against prior statements. Briefly, they produce projects which consist of more than one sentence. (See also Schegloff (1982:74) who calls such a turn a 'discourse')

Reading Sacks et al. closely we find that such a larger project is also called a turn because a turn may consist of a series of sentential unit-types. But how can a speaker who initiates a story bring this story to an end when his co-conversationalists may self select at the first possible completion point of the current turn-constructional unit? This problem is also addressed by Sacks who states: "A problem for parties talking in conversation is how they go about signalling that some utterance that they're producing will or will not be complete on its 'first possible completion'; which is relevant to telling the other that they should or should not be prepared to start talking on a first possible completion. If there is a rule - as I argue there is - that says 'First possible completion can be treated as actual completion', where by 'first possible completion' I mean completion of a first possible sentence; then it is a problem for parties to produce multi-clause sentences. It's a problem that they solve by indicating within the first clause of their intendedly multi-clause sentence, that this is but the first clause, that a second clause will follow." (Sacks W'1970, L2:13-14).

In this quotation, Sacks implicitly indicates that an utterance is not an object which is only syntactically defined. And as will be clear later on he will show that conversationalists also use semantic-pragmatic knowledge when producing and recognizing that an utterance will not be actually completed on its first possible syntactic completion point.

As has been pointed out in the last section such a pragmatic perspective fails in the description of the turn-taking model per se although it should be added that in working out and further explaining this model such a perspective is present to a certain extent.

In Houtkoop & Mazeland (1982, 1985) an attempt has been made to provide for this missing link in the turn-taking model, and to describe which type of knowledge conversationalists use in completing a larger project. Conversationalists are seen as intending to produce so-called 'Discourse Units', or 'DU's' for short, units such as a story, a joke, a countering of an argument, a complaint, and the like. Often such units will take more than just one sentence. There are two types of DU's: Closed and Open DU's. Closed DU's are units with a recognizable beginning and end such as stories or jokes. Open DU's lack a recognizable structure that projects what is to be produced to complete the unit-in-progress. A speaker of an Open DU projects only that there is more to come after this sentence. For example, by saying "I'd like to make two remarks", the speaker indicates that his turn will not be complete before the second answer will have been produced.

With respect to the description of Closed DU's some work by Labov, Sacks, and Jefferson has been of insight. Labov (1972a) describes the structure of stories, and states that they are constructed of sections. A story begins with the 'abstract' in which the reason-for-telling may be indicated. There is the 'orientation-section' in which the place, time, protagonists, etc. of the event to be related, are introduced. The story ends with the 'resolution-section' which may be followed by a 'coda' in which the events told are brought back to the there-and-then. The abstract is of special importance for the discussion of Closed DU's, because it gives an indication of what to expect from the storyteller as he tells his story. The resolution-section and the coda provide indications that the DU, i.e. the story is about to draw to a close.

Sacks and Jefferson worked on stories from a different perspective. Whereas Labov studied stories as structural objects, Sacks and Jefferson took the productional viewpoint (cf. Sacks 1970, L5:17 on the difference between 'story features' and 'story-telling features'). Sacks (F'1966,L3:4 and W'1969,L9:10) points out that speakers who intend to tell a story may use a 'story preface' with which they reserve the floor to tell the multi-utterance unit which the story consists of. Jefferson (1978a) shows how storytellers begin their stories by using a 'story entry device' whereas they use a 'story ending device' to close the story down. With the 'telling ending device' they terminate the telling of the story. As with stories a joke is also preceded by a preface in which the joketeller provides a general characteristic of the joke to come (Sacks 1974). Furthermore Sacks has pointed out that stories and jokes are often told in series. 'Second' and 'next' stories and jokes are heard by reference to the preceding one implying that, once a story or joke has been told, a second one can be told without being prefaced (Sacks S'1967, L7:5 and F'1968, L2:1-31). Besides stories and jokes, there are the fairy-tales with their characteristic beginning ("Once upon a time"), which in the same way project a series of utterances.

So tellers of jokes, stories, and fairy-tales make use of a device to project a larger or 'multi-utterance turn' which has a recognizable last and completing utterance of which the first possible completion point can be treated as the actual completion point of this turn.

Having concluded that conversationalists may produce turns consisting of several sentences we must ask how the turn-taking model can account for the fact that a story-teller can tell a story until its end when a next speaker may self-select on completion of each successive sentence of which the story is built up? When the turn-constructional components are defined pragmatically, rather than syntactically, the problem would seem to be solved. In that case, a story entry device or a joke preface is a turn-constructional unit which projects a 'multi-utterance turn' with a recognizable last utterance. For example, when a speaker produces "Once upon a time" which is recognizable as the first component of a structured series of utterances, he may be heard as initiating a DU, i.e. a fairy-tale. He projects a series of next same-speaker utterances of which one utterance will be the recognizable 'DU-completing utterance'. It may be clear that there are types of Closed DU's: fairy-tales, stories, jokes, etc. which differ in structure and general type of content as well as in the type of the last DU-component.

Now once a speaker has produced a DU-initial utterance all the next utterances prior to the DU-completing one, are heard as DU-incompleting utterances of which the first possible completion points are not to be treated as actual completion points [3], and therefore not as 'proper' transition-relevance places. 'Proper' because on syntactic completion of such an utterance a co-participant is only entitled to produce a 'restricted turn', a turn by which speakership is not taken over.

Although a DU is produced by one participant this does not imply that he will speak continuously until the end of his DU. When he is telling a story his recipient may take turns to express 'story-recipient reactions' (cf. Jefferson 1978a:244). But the recipient is not expected to take a turn to start a DU himself as long as the current DU has not yet been completed [4].

So far Closed DU's have been discussed. However conversationalists also produce Open DU's, which are not so well structured they project a clearly recognizable last component. Still there are ways by which a speaker may indicate that the current utterance will not be the entire intended turn. Like Closed DU's Open DU's may be prefaced.

There is a great deal of literature on prefaces, i.e. turns which preface the action to follow: pre-requests and pre-invitations (Sacks Oct.31, 1967, L8), pre-questions (Schegloff 1980), pre-announcements (Terasaki 1976), and the like. Such prefaces project that the same speaker's next turn will be a request, an invitation, etc., and in doing so they also project a turn which will not be completed as long as the projected action has not yet been produced. In this way prefaces may be used to project a DU. A preface may also be prefaced by a 'preliminary-to-a-preliminary' or a 'pre-pre' (Schegloff 1980). A pre-pre such as "May I ask you a question?" paves the way for a pre-sequence and thus for the action prefaced by this pre-sequence.

Rather than projecting a certain type of next action, a speaker may use a list-initiating marker to project a definite number of next actions, for example, "Let me say two things about it". He may also project an indefinite number of actions to follow, e.g. by saying "Let me give some examples". In such a case the speaker may make use of a list-format (cf. Jefferson (fc)) to signal incompletion of the turn-in-progress, and to signal that the last component is to come now: "and last but not least", or a turn-format like "X, Y and Z".

Furthermore Sacks (W'1970, L2) discusses the use of what he calls 'first verbs' which indicate that more will follow. He illustrates this with "wanted to", a verb of which recipients know that this will be followed by not having managed to do what one wanted to do. In Sacks' example: "The coloured lady wanted to go in the main entrance, and they wouldn't let her go in.". Jefferson (1978b) gives an example of first/second verbs in discussing the "At first I thought X, and then I realized that Y"-construction.

First and second verbs are related to 'contrast classes' (Sacks S'1968, May 29:20-22). Conversationalists make oppositions: if-then clauses, then-now clauses, concessive-adversative clauses, true-false statements, joy-sorrow, etc. In producing the first member of a contrast-pair a speaker projects the second member. This means that a recipient must analyze the utterance in which such an item occurs for the possibility of this item being the first member of a contrast-pair. In the next fragment speaker M. uses the Dutch concessive-adversative "wel-maar"-construction. The conversationalists talk about P's new job:

(6) [HH:TC:12:7]
M. I think it's an incredibly, unbelievably
heavy job.
((some lines omitted))
P. We:ll nice. [I guess.
→ M. [Sure, very nice, but uh with
incre:dibly many hooks and eyes.

It may furthermore be noted that once a first item of a contrast-class has been used the speaker does not need to produce the next part right away. By using such an item he can reserve the floor until the second part has been produced which gives him the chance producing several other utterances before the projected second part.

It may be concluded it is clear that not only syntactic features, but also semantic-pragmatical features which provide a basis for what Sacks (1971, Ch.4:4) calls 'completion detection analysis' of sentences-in-progress, and consequently are a basis for turn-taking.

3.3 Adjacency pairs

Earlier I discussed how during their production utterances may project what may come before their possible completions. This projection-capacity may also hold for what a next speaker is expected to do when the current utterance will be completed.

In the mid-sixties Sacks developed the concept of adjacency pairs, paired classes of utterances, such as question-answer, request-granting/rejection, invitation-acceptance/refusal, greeting-return greeting, etc. Following Schegloff & Sacks (1973), an adjacency pair may be defined as:

1. a sequence of two utterances, which are
2. adjacently ordered, and
3. produced by different speakers;
4. ordered as a first pair-part and a second pair-part
5. and typed, so that a first pair-part makes the occurrence of the second pair-part expectable.

The adjacency pair operates in such a way that "given the recognizable production of a first pair part, on its first possible completion its speaker should stop and a next speaker should start and produce a second pair part from the pair type the first pair part is recognizably a member of." (op.cit.:239). So for example, a question requires an answer, a greeting requires a return-greeting, etc.

This concept is not viewed as a description of an empirical generalization of how first pair-parts will be followed by their second pair-parts. The adjacency pair structure is primarily seen as a "normative framework for actions which is accountably implemented" (Heritage 1984a:247). The concept describes the structural organization of conversation which shapes the expectation and understanding of how actions are organized. When a speaker produces a question he expects to get an answer; and when the addressed party does not give the answer it is said to be 'noticeably absent' (Sacks Nov.15,1971, Ch.2:23). The first speaker will then see the absence of the answer as an accountable event, and will search for the reason of the absence. Atkinson & Drew (1979) point out that e.g., a question is often repeated when the answer does not follow by which the recipient gets a next chance to respond. In the example below when the recipient does not answer at the first opportunity, the speaker solicits an answer twice: firstly with an alternative choice for answers, secondly with a proto-typical prompt object, both based on an analysis presupposing that the recipient heard the original question:

(7) [BR:CM. From Atkinson & Drew 1979:52]
A. Is there something bothering you or not?
(1.0)
→ A. Yes or no.
(1.5)
→ A. Eh?
B. No.

The second pair-part is also called a second or relevant next action to the first action. In producing a relevant next action the recipient displays his understanding of the prior action and defines it as belonging to a certain pair-type. For example, the utterance "Do you smoke?", may be taken as a first pair-part of a Yes/No question-answer pair ("No, I don't"), or of an offer-acceptance/refusal pair ("No, thanks"). Schegloff & Sacks point out that the production of a first pair-part projects a slot for a filler, i.e. a first pair-part is sequentially implicative for the production of its related second part: "By 'sequential implicativeness' is meant that an utterance projects for the sequentially following turn(s) the relevance of a determinate range of occurrences (be they utterance types, activities, speaker selections, etc.). It thus has sequentially organized implications." (Schegloff & Sacks 1973:239).

So utterances or actions may be organized into units, i.e. into sequences. The term sequence "refers to events that occur as a "serial unit", which belong together and follow one after another. They do not happen to occur one after another", as Jefferson (1972:304) circumscribes the term. Once a first part of a sequence has been produced the second will be required to complete the sequence. "When one utterance (or member of a class of utterances) is conditionally relevant on another, or when one action is conditionally relevant on another, attention is called to their treatment by members as a "sequence" in the strong sense. Given the occurrence of the first, the second is expectable; upon its occurrence it is seen (analyzed) by members as the second to the first, as the second part, as produced 'responsively'", as Schegloff (1967:32) formulates it.

The fact that a second pair-part is next-positioned to a first pair-part does not necessarily mean that it will occur right after the first. In other words an utterance being next-positioned does not necessarily mean being next-located. An utterance or action is next-positioned when it is a response to a prior utterance or action. But between the first and second part may occur other utterances. These in-between-utterances may form an 'insertion sequence' (Sacks F'1966,L4), as in the following example:

(8) [Merritt 1976:333]

	A. May I have a bottle of Mich	(question 1)
→	B. Are you twenty one?	(question 2)
→	A. No.	(answer 2)
	B. No.	(answer 1)

The four turns are adjacently located, i.e. they occur one after the other. But the first and second pair-parts of the request-rejection sequence are not adjacently located, they are intersected by a question-answer sequence. The main sequence-parts however, are adjacently positioned. As Levinson (1983) points out 'turn-location' refers to the location of a turn after an initial turn, whereas 'turn-position' refers to the response to a preceding turn, but not necessarily the adjacently placed turn. So a second pair-part separated from its first part by an insertion sequence, will be found in the fourth turn but in second sequence-position. A sequential structure then holds across a sequence of positions rather than across a sequence of turns. So answers and other second pair-parts are next-positioned items, and they are understood by reference to a preceding unit (see Sacks F'1967,L13 and L14 on next-positionedness). By virtue of this next-positioned character of second pair-parts, we can hear the first "No" in the preceding fragment as the answer to the question "Are you twenty one?", whereas the second "No" is a response to "May I have a bottle of Mich".

Moreover a strong preference for contiguity exists (Sacks 1973:9). When a speaker produces two questions in one turn, and the recipient produces two answers to this turn, the order of the answers will be the reverse of the order of the questions. For example:

(9) [Sacks 1973:9]

Q1. A. Well that's good uh how <u>is</u> yer arthritis.
Q2 A. Yuh still takin shots?
A2 B. Yeah.
A1 B. Well it's, it's <u>awright</u> I mean it's uh,
it hurts once 'n while but <u>it's</u> okay.

3.3.1 On the two-part structure of adjacency pairs

In the preceding section I discussed adjacency pairs which are by definition two-part sequences. In some literature (e.g. Appel et al. 1976, Weijdema et al. 1982, Severinson Eklundh & Linell 1983, Goffman 1976), it has been suggested however, that these sequences consist perhaps more often of three parts than of two. The initial speaker is supposed to have the right to produce a next utterance in response to recipient's second-positioned utterance. Goffman says that "a response will on occasion leave matters in a ritually unsatisfactory state, and a turn by the initial speaker will be required, encouraged, or at least allowed, resulting in a three-part interchange; or chains of adjacency pairs will occur (...), the chain itself having a unitary bounded character." (Goffman 1976:25).

In the following I will support this view, and some empirical evidence will be given. The consequence of the view of adjacency pairs basically being three part sequences, is that proposal-acceptance sequences will now be treated as initiative-response-acknowledgement sequences.

Before discussing the three-part character of these sequences I will pay some attention to the literature on institutional interaction since this three-part structure has been described especially in the literature on, for example, classroom interaction and doctor-patient interaction.

Coulthard (1977), Mehan (1979), and earlier Sinclair and Coulthard (1975), discuss such a three-part structure in classroom interaction:

1 teacher:	initiative	(known-answer question)
2 pupil :	response	(answer)
3 teacher:	follow up	(evaluation)

The initiating action is a so-called known-answer question, a question which is meant to check the pupil's knowledge, and of which the teacher knows the correct answer. The sequential implicativeness of the third-positioned evaluation [5] is said to be so strong that, if the teacher does not evaluate the answer, the answer is treated by the pupils as incorrect.

Wells et al. (1979) discuss the existence of this three-part sequence type in mother-child interaction when mothers ask the same kind of known-answer questions (or 'display questions' as Wells et al. call them) to their children, and where the answer is evaluated.

Three-part sequences are also said to occur in doctor-patient interaction. Fisher (1984) talks about the 'initiation act-reply act-evaluation act', and the 'initiation act-response act-comment act'. "A speech act initiated by one participant is followed by a response by the other, which on some occasions is followed by a comment act." (op.cit:204-5). Fisher says about this three-part structure that: "This sequential organization is more similar to the three part structure found in classroom interaction than it is to the two part structure found in everyday conversations. Like discourse in classrooms, it is shaped by the institutional setting in which it occurs and the practical concerns of the participants. In the medical setting, the sequential organization into initiation, response, and comment sequences (I-R-C) is influenced by the need to exchange information upon which treatment decisions will be reached." (Fisher 1984:205).

In this quotation Fisher suggests that two-part sequences are typical for everyday conversation, and that they may turn into three-part sequences in institutional interaction. Other authors however, suggest the reverse to a certain extent. Third-turn receipts are often absent in institutional interactions (e.g. in news interviews; cf. Heritage 1985), or they are of a limited type (e.g. in courtroom interaction; cf. Atkinson 1982). Frankel (1984) and Ten Have (1986) make similar remarks with respect to medical interactions. Frankel (1984) for example, distinguishes between assessments (containing contrast class terms such as good/bad, right/wrong etc.), and acknowledgement third turn-types (containing neutral terms such as "Okay", "I see". etc.). He found that only 2.9% of the 675 sequences with some form of third-turn additions contained assessment terms, whereas 61.6% of the time the third turns contained neutral terms. When comparing this result with Mehan's finding that teachers always use the third turn to assess the student's answers, Frankel points to the difference in the goals and criteria of performance for medical and classroom interaction: "A physician's major task in the beginning of an encounter is to obtain enough information to make sound clinical judgements about a patient's medical concern(s). Completeness of information gathered from the patient is thus paramount in the decision making process. A teacher's major task in directing classroom instruction is to judge the propositional content of student answers according to standards tacitly understood by all to be known in advance. In the classroom, it is the correctness of an answer that counts." (Frankel 1984:157).

Next I will show that there are good reasons for questioning the typicality of adjacency pairs being two-part sequences in everyday conversation. It will be argued that most types of adjacency pairs are to be seen as adjacency triplets. An important reason to discuss this point to some extent is that the remote proposal sequence will be discussed later on as a five-part sequence of which the fifth sequence-part is similar to the third-turn receipt.

Perhaps since adjacency pairs are discussed in the CA-literature from the perspective of the relationship between first and second pair-parts, the idea of these pairs being two-part sequences seems to be taken for granted, not to be questioned anymore. Over and over again authors talk about adjacency pairs, and as far as they provide illustrations these illustrations seem to confirm this two-part structure. For example, in Levinson 1983:304 we find:

(10) [Merritt 1976:333]
A. May I have a bottle of Mich?
((insertion sequence omitted))
B. No.

Or in Schegloff 1972:78,

(11) A. Are you coming tonight?
((insertion sequence omitted))
B. I'll be there.

The authors provide such fragments up to the second pair-part of the sequence. But one wonders what happens right after the recipients' responses. And reading other fragments given by the same authors one finds three-part sequences indeed, for example, in Levinson's discussion of pre-requests (I have underlined the acknowledgement of the response):

(12) [Levinson 1983:347]
C. Do you have the blackberry jam?
S. Yes.
C. <u>Okay</u>. Can I have half a pint then?
S. Sure. ((turns to get))

and on page 358 he quotes:

(13) [Merritt 1976:325]
C. Do you have Marlboros?
S. Uh, no. We ran out.
C. <u>Okay.</u> Thanks anyway.

S. Sorry.

In these fragments the first speakers acknowledge the prior responses. But due to the manner in which the fragments are reproduced here, it looks as though the second pair-part is immediately followed by a new initiation. It may be the case that the assumption of the existence of adjacency pairs as two-part sequences has led to a selective perception and thereby to a selective way of presenting examples and segmenting fragments.

Although none of the CA authors explicitly addresses the question of adjacency pairs as probable three-part sequences, some of them describe such structures and make observations in this direction. Sacks states that the speaker of a first part "has the reserved right to talk again." (Sacks S'1966, L2:9). This seems to return in Sacks et al. (1978:45) as the 'last-as-next-speaker-bias'. Jefferson (1981b:25) goes a little further in saying that, since the first speaker has the right to speak again after the second part, an inquiry sets up a three-part sequence.

Heritage (1984a) refers to the first speaker's right to talk again after the response as the 'third-turn option'. He mentions this in the framework of his discussion of how a co-participant displays his analysis of a prior utterance in the response to that utterance.

One third-turn option which is open to the first speaker is the explicit correction, or repair, of a misunderstanding which was displayed in the second speaker's turn. That is, it gives the first speaker the opportunity to indicate that the response given was not the one looked for, or was a misunderstanding of the first turn, and hence a third-turn repair. The producer of a first action "has a systematically given opportunity to repair any misunderstanding of the first action that may have been displayed in the second.", as Heritage (1984a:258) says.

For example in the next fragment (fabricated by Heritage), the initial speaker uses the third-turn option to display that the recipient has misunderstood the sense of the initial utterance:

(14) [Heritage 1984a:258]
     B. Why don't you come and <u>see</u> me
        some [times.
     A.   [I would like to
→   B. Yes but why <u>don't</u> you

It needs to be pointed out here that, since this third turn is a new initiation, Heritage does not treat it as a third turn in a sequence; it is only a third turn in a series of turns. And concluding from the next quotation, this third-turn option is not to be used by the first speaker to display the second speaker's adequate treatment of the first turn: "Given the generic availability of this procedure, any second speaker may look to a third action to see whether this opportunity was taken and, if it was not, conclude that the analysis and treatment of the first action that was displayed in his or her second was adequate." (op.cit.:258). Heritage thus appears to maintain the idea that a first action sets up a two-part sequence rather than a three-part sequence. Interestingly enough however, the fabricated fragment given earlier is a revision of a fragment which looks like a adjacency triplet:

(15) [SBL:10:12. From Schegloff 1972:107)
B. Why don't you come and <u>see</u> me
some [times
A. [I would like to.
→ B. I would like you to.

In this fragment we find a first speaker's acknowledgement of the second turn. Similar examples are given by Sacks (March 5, 1969, L9) when he discusses 'third utterances' such as:

(16) [Sacks 1969]
A. How long are you gonna be in town?
B. Uh, till about Monday.
→ A. Oh it'll be just a week then.

(17) [Sacks 1969]
A. Where are you staying?
B. In Pacific Pallisades.
→ A. Oh on the west side of town.

These utterances, which follow a question-answer sequence, have as their specific function that the first speaker, as Sacks says, shows his understanding of the prior answer. And it is clear that these first speakers use the third-turn option to display that they have understood the prior utterance rather than to initiate a correction or repair.

In fact to show understanding of the answer is not all there is to say about the function of the third turns or third-turn receipts, they also evaluate the adequacy of the answer. This does not only hold for institutional interaction ('correct answers' in classroom interaction or 'complete answers' in medical interaction, cf. Frankel 1984:157), but also for everyday conversation. A question does not simply require just an answer but a specific answer. For example, the question of how old the recipient is seeks for an answer such as "38 years old", "I'm your age", or the like. In the next fragment such a question is being posed:

(18) [HH:TC:11:2]
→ T. How old are you?
A. Well uh I'>m not thirty yet<.
((some lines omitted))
(1.0)
T. Gh(h). How- how old then?
A. Hahahaha. I(h)'m no(h)t thi(h)rty yet.
Ga-ha:. No I(h)'m twe(h)nty-ni(h)ne.=
T. =You're not in television.
(1.7)
T. Interview this.

In response to "How old are you?", T. indicates that she is "not thirty yet". This is not an adequate answer to this question. When A. finally mentions her age, after she has been prompted by T's "How- how old then?", the initial question has been 'fulfilled' (Wunderlich 1976).

These fragments therefore support the assumption that a first action may set up a three-part sequence of which the third sequence-position is open to some sort of reaction by the first speaker. Such a type of reaction may also be an acknowledgement. Schegloff for example, states that "if X takes a position, and Y then states a position intended to show, rather than claim, agreement with X's position, then X should acknowledge agreement to show his appreciation that Y was showing agreement" (Schegloff 1984:42). This then sets up the adjacency triplet:

1 speaker : assertion
2 recipient: showing agreement
3 speaker : acknowledgement i.e. showing appreciation

Particularly in cases of initial utterances formulated as interrogatives, it makes sense to have the structural provision of a third-turn option. Interrogatives are used for different sorts of initial actions: inquiries, requests, invitations, known-answer questions, pre-announcements, story- and joke-prefaces, etc. And since interrogatives may be 'sequentially ambiguous' [6] (cf. Sacks Oct.24,1967), it is important that a first speaker has the opportunity to signal whether a second speaker has treated the first turn according to the first speaker's intentions.

Heritage (1984a) also points out the relevance of the third-turn option referring to the following example of a so-called correction sequence (Jefferson 1972). Three children are playing a game; Steven is age 6, Nancy and Susan age 8:

(19) [Jefferson 1972:295]

Steven: One, two, three, ((pause)) four, five,
six, ((pause)) eleven, eight nine ten.
Susan : "Eleven"?-eight, nine, ten?
Steven: Eleven, eight, nine, ten?
Nancy : "Eleven"?
Steven: Seven, eight, nine, ten.
Susan : That's better.
((whereupon the game resumes))

In this fragment Susan solicits from Steven a correction to his prior utterance. When he makes the same mistake again Nancy solicits him to correct it. Then when Steven produces the correction, Susan acknowledges this by "That's better." This correction sequence consists of the three parts:

(correctable item)
1 correction solicitor
2 correction
3 acknowledgement i.e. affirmation

It may be mentioned here that Jefferson talks about a four-part sequence because she takes the correctable item, which precedes the correction solicitor as the first part of this sequence. However I take it as a three-part sequence. Given that any item in talk can be treated in theory as a correctable, then any item might be an initial action in a correction sequence. Since it is only the correction solicitor which reveals that an error was made, only correction solicitors initiate or mobilize a correction sequence; the indefinite number of possibilities for correction are only realized in and through correction solicitors. Heritage then says that the "that's better" acknowledgement demonstrates that the preceding ""Eleven"? -eight, nine ten?", and ""Eleven"?" have been known-answer questions, i.e. questions of which the questioners know the correct answer. An acknowledgement such as "Oh" on the other hand demonstrates that the preceding interrogative has been a 'real question' in the sense of Searle (1969:67), and that the information provided by the answerer is new to recipient. Heritage refers to such an "Oh" as a 'change-of-state token', a term which refers to the fact that the producer of the "Oh" signals to have undergone some kind of change in his locally current state of knowledge (Heritage 1984b:299).

Heritage analyzed data in which the solicited response is acknowledged by such an "Oh". It turned out that several types of second actions may be acknowledged by an "Oh", for example, the other-initiated repair sequence (to be compared with Jefferson's correction sequence).

(repairable item)
1 repair initiation
2 repair
3 acknowledgement i.e. "Oh"-receipt

For example :

```
(20) [NB:111:1:2. From Heritage 1984b:318]
     F. When didju want'er thih come do::w[n.
     S.                                   [.hhh Oh
        any time between: now en nex' Saturday, hh
     F. A wee:k from:: (0.3) this coming Saturdee.
     S. Yeah.
           (.)
-->  F. .hhh Oh:::.
```

Heritage takes this sequence as a four-part sequence. For the same reasons as given above I take it as a three-part sequence.

Also the understanding check-confirmation/disconfirmation sequence can be followed by an "Oh":

(repairable item)
1 understanding check
2 confirmation/disconfirmation
3 acknowledgement i.e."Oh" receipt

For example:

```
(21) [Rah:11:7. From Heritage 1984b:319]
     J. Derek's ho:me?
          (0.5)
     I. Yo:ur De[rek.
     J.         [Ye:s m[m.
-->  I.                [Oh:.
```

The same holds for question-answer sequences:

1 question
2 answer
3 acknowledgement

for example:

```
(22) [TC11(b):28]
     P. D'yih know'r Mister Bodwin i:s.
        ((some lines omitted))
     B. No:.
 →   P. Oh okay,
```

Jefferson & Schenkein (1977) describe another three-part sequence, the 'appeal sequence':

1 appeal
2 acceptance/rejection
3 acknowledgement.

They give the following fragment in which a salesboy tries to convince Michael and Steven to subscribe to a newspaper:

```
(23) [Jefferson & Schenkein 1977]
     Salesboy: Would any of you other gentlemen be
               innerested.
               ((pause))
     Salesboy: Dju be innerested sir, ((addressed to
               Michael))
               ((Pause))
     Salesboy: Taking the Progress Bulletin,
     Steven  : No, en he don' know nothin about it
 →   Salesboy: Okay.
```

Jefferson (1972:317) speaks of such an "Okay" as an object which signals 'satisfactory termination'. It may be added to this that, more generally speaking, acknowledgements function as 'sequence exit devices' (Heritage 1984b:318), and thus pave the way for a new sequence and activity.

So far we have seen some types of first pair-parts of which the response is acknowledged by first speaker. However this phenomenon seems to be much more general. It also occurs after, at least, question-answer sequences, request-acceptance sequences, offer-acceptance sequences, and proposal-acceptance sequences. In the following I will show some Anglo-American as well as Dutch fragments where preferred responses to different types of first actions (see 3.4) are acknowledged by the initial speaker. The three sequence positions are numbered, and the acknowledgement is arrowed.

Over and over again we find the following structure:

```
1 speaker  : initiation
2 recipient: response
3 speaker  : sequence closing/acknowledgement
```

First the response to a question or inquiry will be acknowledged:

```
(24) [HH:TC:18:2]
        K. U:h Kees Koster speaking
        H. Hi: Kees.
      1 K. Were you already in bed?
      2 H. Oh no.
 →    3 K. O(h)o(h)o.

(25) [HG:11:1. From Button & Casey 1984:172; simplified]
        H. Hwaryuhh=
        N. =Fi:ne=
      1 N. how'r you,
                (.)
      2 H. Oka:[y,
 →    3 N.     [Goo:d,
```

In the following fragment we find a series of question-answer sequences again. This fragment shows that on completion of a sequence a new (perhaps related), topic may be introduced, as pointed out earlier. The new topic will be double arrowed.

```
(26) [HH:TC:11:1]
        A. Ja, this is Ageeth Snabel?
                (0.4)
        T. Hello:, it's Ton, Ageeth.
        A. Ja hello.
        T. Hello.
      1 T. Are you guys sitting on the balcony?
                (0.4)
      2 A. .hh No:, we are u:h watching television.
 →    3 T. Oh gosh.
 →→   1 T. What's on?
                (0.3)
      2 A. .hh no(h)thing. The ne:ws.
 →    3 T. Oh, the news. O:h.
 →→   1 T. Can you do without?=
```

2 A. =.hh Ja no we're getting older. No uh I
can do without. Sure.
→ 3 T. Oh.
→→ 1 T. You're u::h back from your holidays?

After the initial speaker acknowledges the solicited response the topic is changed or shifted from 'what are you guys doing', via 'what's on television', and changed [7] from 'can you do without', to 'you're back from your holidays'.

Also the acceptance of a request is acknowledged:

(27) [HH:TC:20:2]
1 C. May I speak to Aletta please?
(0.3)
2 A. Ja:.
→ 3 C. Okay::.

This request is a request by caller to speak to someone else. When the request has been accepted the caller acknowledges the acceptance, after which the answerer calls the required person to the telephone (in 4.1 more will be said about this type of request.)

We also find an acknowledgement of the acceptance of an offer or proposal:

(28) [HH:TC:22:10]
1 A. Should I get her for you?
2 C. Ja:, if uh (.) if possible, ja.=
→ 3 A. =Okay.
((A calls her))

In the following fragment the acceptance of an order or instruction is acknowledged:

(29) [HH:TC:30:40]
1 B. Do not confirm. ((the flight))
2 A. No:, fine.
(0.5)
→ 3 B. O:kay.

In all these fragments the initial speakers acknowledge the responses. Such an acknowledgement functions on two levels of the interaction. It treats the preceding response as being informative ("Oh"), surprising ("Oh gosh") or agreed on ("Ja. Fine"), or more generally speaking it 'accepts' the response as a satisfactory one. On a sequential level the acknowledgement closes off the action sequence, and provides for the initiation of a new activity. In Chapter 4 it will become clear that five-part proposal sequences too, are closed off by such acknowledgement tokens.

In this way sequence-closing utterances play a role in the segmentation of the stream of talk into separate blocks, each block being structurally as well as topically distinct from the preceding and the following one.

That a sequence has a third position for the acknowledgement-utterance does not necessarily mean that this position needs to be filled. The sequence may be closed by initiating a recognizable new action. In the following extract the acknowledgement is absent, and after a pause of 0.7 seconds (which provides room for such an acknowledgement; cf. Maynard 1980 on such pauses), a new action is begun:

(30) [HH:TC:12:1]
1 F. Hey, will you be coming too?
M. Where?
F. Here?
2 M. Oh that's alright.
→ (0.7)
→ M. No, what I actually wanted to know,
because uh (.) is Elly there?

When the closing item is not produced the sequence can be closed by opening a next activity. In this fragment the new utterance begins in such a way that M. signals that 'something else', i.e. a topic unrelated to the prior one is being initiated. The question "Is Elly there?", is preceded by a 'topic-transitional utterance' (Sacks S'1971, April 12:4-6.) "No, what I actually wanted to know". Such a topic-transitional utterance has a retrospective-prospective function it opens a new topic and by virtue of that, it closes the preceding topic and sequence.

In order to avoid going into too much detail, irrelevant for the core of the present research, let it suffice to say that after having received a response the initial speaker may continue in the following three ways.

The speaker may a) acknowledge the response before going on to produce a new action as in:

(31) [SBL:3:3:6]
1 M. The- Your leg (got) alright huh,
2 K. Oh yeah.
3 M. Oh good.
→ M. Tell Keith Moon hello for me.

or b), speaker may use the response for further topical

development as in:

```
(32) [SBL:2:1:6:R]
     1 B. Dih you know wut La:zy Daisy cake i:s?
     2 T. YE::s=
→      B. =.hh We:ll? I used tha:t, an' (...)
```

or c) the initial speaker may not react at all, after which the recipient will extend his response, an example of that being:

```
(33) [HER:ol:18:r:SO. Simplified]
     1 N. How are you feeling.
     2 D. Oh I feel fine?
→            (1.0)
→      D. Absolutely fine?
     3 N. Y:ou do.
              (.)
       N. Alright. You had a good slee:p?
```

Important is for the argument of adjacency pairs being in fact basically three-part sequences this last example where the initial speaker does not react when the recipient has responded to the question, upon which the recipient extends her response-utterance. She thus solicits the speaker to acknowledge her response. This indicates that conversationalists are normatively oriented to the response being acknowledged by the initial speaker.

The main point therefore, is not the fact that these sequences as such have a three-part structure. The important feature is that the co-participant who solicits a response will also let his recipient know what he thinks of that response, and whether it was what he was looking for when producing the question or the request. When Heritage says that initial speakers have a third-turn option in order to be able to initiate a repair in case the response has not been satisfactory, he is right, but in addition initial speakers should also have the opportunity to demonstrate the initiation has been correctly responded to. And as it turns out initial speakers not only have this opportunity, but they are normatively oriented to the initial speaker taking this opportunity.

In Chapter 4 I will continue and show that requests or offers concerning the immediate execution of some action set up a three-part sequence as discussed here. When however, they concern an action to be executed some time later they set up a five-part sequence which is also closed off by the conversationalist who has initiated the sequence. The structure is basically the same as the one discussed before except that between the response and the sequence-closing acknowledgement an extra sequence is built in, where co-participants can deal with the special requirements of this special type of action.

3.3.2 Adjacency pairs versus reciprocal pairs

Since adjacency pairs have been at stake here some further remarks may be made briefly. Schegloff & Sacks (1973) say that the two utterances of an adjacency pair are ordered as a first and a second pair-part, and they are typed so that the first pair-part makes the production of the second relevant. A good example of this is the question-answer pair. The question provides a slot for the answer. It is important here that the question necessarily precedes the answer, and not the other way around. The same holds for requests, invitations, or offers, which necessarily precede the acceptance or rejection.

While this is basic for adjacency pairs there is a problem with two sequence-types which are traditionally seen as adjacency pairs as well, i.e. identification sequences and greeting sequences, especially as they occur in Dutch telephone conversations.

In contrast to American telephone conversations (cf. Schegloff 1967, 1979, 1986), Dutch telephone conversations have as their typical opening sequence (cf. Houtkoop-Steenstra 1986b):

```
((ringing of the telephone))
Answerer: self-identification
Caller  : self-identification
Answerer: greeting
Caller  : greeting
```

For example:

```
(34) [HH:TC:12:1]
     Answerer: Catherijne speaking?
                   (0.7)
     Caller  : Martijn speaking.
                   (0.5)
     Answerer: Hi=
     Caller  : =Hi.
```

The main difference is that whereas American conversationalists preferably use a voice-sample ("Hello?"), to be recognized by co-participant ("Hi!", or "John!"), Dutch telephone conversationalists both self-identify by mentioning their names. And since the called/answerer is the one to speak first (Sacks S'1967,L2:4; Schegloff 1979), he is the first one to self-identify, followed by the caller self-identifying. Given the rule that speakership is allocated and the rule of one-speaker-at-a-time it follows that when the caller has self-identified the answerer may make a greeting after which the caller may do the same.

The conversation will be terminated by a "Bye bye"-exchange:

(35) [HH:TC:20:39]
Answerer: Martijn, see you.
Caller : Okay::.
→ Answerer: [Bye bye:.
→ Caller : [Bye bye:.

These sequences consist of two parts [8], but strictly speaking this does not make them adjacency pairs. Although the two turns occur one after the other they cannot be characterized as the first and the second parts of a pair in the way of question-answer sequences or request-acceptance sequences, where the two parts cannot be interchanged. Goffman (1971) discusses these sequences from a different perspective. He speaks of 'interpersonal verbal rituals', which mark daily activities: "Sleep well", "Good morning", or "Hello-Hello". Goffman sees such an exchange as a response to this situation instead of seeing a secondly produced "Hello" as the response to an initially produced "Hello". It can be added that as far as a greeting or an identification occurs as the first of two greetings or identifications it is only the product of the conversationalists having applied some conversational rules, i.e. answerer-speaks-first-rule and the one-speaker-at-a-time-rule. The two items may as well be produced in the reverse order, or they may be produced almost or entirely simultaneously [9]. This happens in the preceding fragment as well as in:

(36) [Her:01:13]
Heath: A:'right,
Nan : See you,
Heath: °°Yes. [Bye °°
Nan : [Bye:,

Although identifications will not easily be produced simultaneously their order of production is free. Although this is not the normative rule in Dutch telephone conversations the caller may be the first to identify himself, for example:

(37) [HH:TC:21:034]
Answerer: Ja Hallo:.
→ Caller : Hallo: this is u:h Ronny. Waldman.
(1.0)
Caller : Of Steelstreet number 47.
(1.0)
Caller : Who is this? Is this u:h
Answerer: U:h this is Patricia:. Jan and Marijke aren't home.

After having mentioned his name Ronny does not receive the name of the answerer, and he extends his identification by providing further details of his identification. When this still has not triggerered o the answerer's self-identification after a pause of 1.0 seconds (cf. Jefferson, 1983b, on the standard maximum silence of approximately 1 second), Ronny explicitly asks for his name, which he then indeed receives. Furthermore the fragment shows that co-participants may be solicited to identify themselves when they have not done so freely. For further instances see Houtkoop-Steenstra (1986b)

Identifications and greetings do come in pairs, and they constitute what I shall call 'reciprocal pairs' [10] (cf. Clark & French 1981 on the "goodbye"-exchange as a 'coordinate pair').

Reciprocal pairs are action sequences:
1 Consisting of two identical actions,
2 which are produced by two (or more) different speakers,
3 such that the two actions may but need not occur one after the other,
4 without them being hierarchically ordered as a first and a second pair-part.

For a more detailed discussion of reciprocal pairs see Houtkoop-Steenstra (1986a).

Without disputing the concept of next-positioned character as the basis of adjacency pairs the adjacency pair as the only kind of sequential ordering has been questioned here. Whereas some of these action sequences have been described as three-part sequences, or as adjacency triplets, others are seen as reciprocal pairs.

3.4 Preference organization

When discussing adjacency pairs it has been mentioned that certain initial actions have two alternatives as their relevant next actions. For example, invitations, proposals, offers, and requests have an acceptance or a rejection as their responses. These two alternative responses are not of equal standing. One of them is preferred, the other is dispreferred; for example, whereas a self-deprecation has as its preferred response a disagreement, a request invites acceptance as the preferred next action. What the preferred next action is is structured in part by the action performed with the initial utterance. The preference status of a second action is associated with the turn shape in which this second action is produced. Therefore the term preference does not refer to the speaker's state of mind and desire, but to the features of the various ways each of the alternatives (i.e. preferred of dispreferred) are organized, both sequentially and in terms of the design of their turns. Preferred and dispreferred responses are formulated in different ways, i.e. they are put into 'preferred' or 'dispreferred-action turn shapes' (Pomerantz 1984a:63). Before discussing this into more detail I will list initial actions that have alternative responses. The first response is the preferred one, the second is the dispreferred one.

initiation	-preferred	/ dispreferred response
proposal	-acceptance	/ rejection
	cf. Davidson 1984	
request	-compliance	/ refusal
	cf. Wootton 1981	
request	-acceptance	/ rejection
	cf. Davidson 1984	
offer	-acceptance	/ rejection
	cf. Davidson 1984	
invitation	-acceptance	/ rejection
	cf. Davidson 1984	
assessment	-agreement	/ disagreement
	cf. Pomerantz 1984a	
self-deprecation	-disagreement	/ agreement
	cf. Pomerantz 1984a	
compliment	-disagreement	/ agreement
	cf. Pomerantz 1978	
question	-expected answer	/ unexpected answer

	cf. Levinson 1983	
laughter	-laughter	/ declination
	cf. Jefferson 1979	
complaint	-agreement	/ disagreement
	cf. Sacks W' 1971	

Note that recipients need not respond with the preferred or dispreferred response. They may also, what I would like to call, 'not-yet-accept' or 'non-accept' a request, 'not-yet-answer' or 'non-answer' a question, etc. For example, in response to a request recipients may defer the solicited response by indicating that they will think it over, or that they will decide tomorrow. Or in response to a question recipients may indicate that they do not know the answer, or that they do not have an opinion on speaker's assertion.

However such a non-response is generally treated as a (potentially) dispreferred response, i.e. a rejection, a disagreement, and the like. That is, it tends to have the sequential consequence of a dispreferred response (cf. Wootton 1981, Pomerantz 1984a, Davidson 1984).

Speakers may design their initial utterances so as to project the preferred response as has been frequently discussed in the linguistic literature (e.g. Lyons, 1977:765 on 'checking tags'; Franck 1980 on the role of modal particles in leading questions in German), as well as in the CA literature (cf. Sacks 1973, Pomerantz 1984a). A strong projection device in English is the tag-question, for example:

(38) [JS:11:28, from Pomerantz 1984a:59]
J. T's-stuh beautiful day out isn't it?
L. Yeh it's just gorgeous...

Whereas English tends to use tag-questions to project an agreeing response, in Dutch (like in German) this is done by means of modal particles such as "zeker", "zeker wel/niet", "toch", "toch wel/niet", a stressed "wel", or by adding the, what might be called tag-questioning particles "hè?", "toch?", or "nietwaar?" (in English e.g."right?") to the utterance. For example:

(39) [HH:TC:18:6]
R. Morgen moet ze ook werken, hè?
K. E::h ja.

→ R. She has to work tomorrow too, right?
K. U::h ja.

In the next fragment the caller projects a "No"-answer

by means of "zeker...niet" ("surely...not"):

(40) [HH:TC:26:10]
C. Uh Ireen is t'r zeker niet?
A. Ja, die is t'r wel.

C. Uh Irene won't be there, will she?
A. Ja, she is there.

The use of the stressed Dutch "wel" in the answer indicates that the recipient also hears the speaker's utterance as projecting a negative response, i.e. that Irene will not be home.

Recipients are normatively oriented to respond to such utterances in agreement with the projected response. Sacks (1973) shows that even when recipients disagree with the prior utterance they tend to design their response in such a way that it still seems to be in agreement with the preference. [11]

A device used frequently is to begin the response-turn by stating (partial) agreement, and then continue to state or to demonstrate disagreement. For example:

(41) [Sacks 1973:6]
A. Well is this really whatchu wanted?
→ B. Uh ... not originally? No. But it's uh ...
promotion? an it's uh very interesting, ...

The question is formulated in such a way that it suggests that "this" is not what the recipient will have wanted really. And the recipient initially agrees: this is not what he wanted "originally", and only then will he make clear that in the mean time this is what he wants, because it is "promotion" and "very interesting". Another example:

(42) [JG:11.1.-15. From Pomerantz 1984a:72]
G. ... you've really both basically
honestly gone your own ways.
→ D. Essentially, except we've hadda
a good relationship et home

Again the recipient begins by agreeing with the prior utterance; the speaker is "essentially" right, but for the exception.

The preference for agreement may explain why in the next fragment, the little girl Kitty only takes a deep breath when the caller supposes that Kitty knows who he is:

(43) [HH:TC:12:47]

M. You know who I am, eh?
K. ((Sighs deeply))
M. Or don't you. Ja:::. Martijn from Rotterdam.
((noises))
K. Ja.

Although the sheer fact that Martijn poses this question displays that he doubts whether Kitty knows to whom she is talking, it nevertheless projects a positive answer; this is due to the declarative formulation of the utterance ("You know who I am") and the tag-question ("eh?"). And whereas it becomes clear for Martijn that Kitty does not know ("Or don't you. Ja:::. Martijn from Rotterdam."), she says "Ja", that is she claims to know who the speaker is. [12]

Sacks (S'1970,L5) makes a distinction between 'claiming' (or 'stating', 'asserting'), and 'showing' (or 'demonstrating'), with respect to the understanding of the prior utterance. Pomerantz (1984a) has discussed this difference with respect to agreement with a prior assertion. In Dutch the initial stating of agreement and the subsequent demonstration of disagreement can be done straightforwardly with the 'consessive-adversative' "wel-maar" construction'. By starting with "Jawel"/ "That's right", or with some longer version of this the recipient states agreement with the prior assertion, and in continuing with "maar"/"but" he demonstrates his disagreement (Houtkoop-Steenstra 1980; see also Pomerantz 1984a on a similar English procedure). This happens in the next fragment where co-participants are discussing P.'s new job. This fragment also contains several other features of a dispreferred response such as delaying the response by a pre-turn pause (line 3), a "We:ll" (line 6) (cf. Driessen & van Mierlo 1984 on the Dutch "nou:"), and a repair-initiator (line 4):

(44) [HH:TC:12:7]

M. I think it will be an incredibly,
unbelievably heavy job.
→ (1.0)
→ P. What? That it's an?
M. An unbelievably heavy job.
→ P. We:ll nice, [I think.
→ M. [Sure, very nice, but uh
with i:ncredibly many hooks and eyes.

When P. says that his new job will be nice M. first agrees, but goes right on to say this is not the issue.

This fragment also shows how a recipient may state some acceptance of a suggestion, and then demonstrate his rejection. As discussed in Houtkoop-Steenstra 1986c the difference between stating and demonstrating also holds for the response to actions such as suggestions, requests, etc. which have an acceptance as their preferred response.

Sacks relates the preference for agreement with a prior utterance to the preference for contiguity, that is the preference for a reponse to start right after the completion of the preceding utterance. This point has been developed by Pomerantz: "(...) an action, by virtue of how the participants orient to it, will be housed in and performed through a turn shape that reflects their orientation. That is, there is an association between an action's preference status and the turn shape in which it is produced." (Pomerantz 1984a:64). Sacks shows that the interaction between the preference for agreement with the preceding utterance or action and the preference for contiguity is such that, if an agreeing response is produced, it tends to occur right on or after completion of the utterance to which it responds. A disagreeing response however, tends to be produced non-contiguously. "It may well be pushed rather deep into the turn that it occupies" (Sacks 1973:7). When agreement is the preferred response, agreement-turns are structured so as to maximize occurrences of stated agreements, whereas disagreement turns are structured such as to minimize stated disagreement as Pomerantz signals.

According to Pomerantz agreement-turns and disagreement-turns have the following characteristics:

1 "Agreements have agreement components occupying the entire agreement turns; disagreements are often prefaced.
2 Agreements are accomplished with stated agreement components; disagreements may be accomplished with a variety of forms, ranging from unstated to stated disagreements. Frequently disagreements, when stated, are formed as partial agreements/partial disagreements; they are weak forms of disagreement.
3 In general, agreements are performed with a minimization of gap between the prior turn's completion and the agreement turn's initiation; disagreement components are frequently delayed within a turn or over a series of turns." (cf. Sacks' preference for contiguity). [Disagreements may be delayed by pre-turn pauses, pre-turn hesitations ("Uh", "well"), stated agreements ("that's right, but..."), appreciations in

case of offers, invitations and the like ("That's very nice of you, but..."), apologies in case of requests and invitations, etc., or they may be delayed by means of repair-initiators.]

4 "Absences of forthcoming agreements or disagreements by recipients with gaps, requests for clarification and the like are interpretable as instances of unstated, or as-yet-unstated, disagreements."
(Pomerantz 1984a:65).

Sangers (1985) reaches the conclusion that the analysis of Pomerantz also holds for Dutch telephone conversation data.

The difference between preferred and dispreferred turn-shapes and the ways in which recipients foreshadow disagreement is important with respect to the analysis of remote proposal sequences to be presented in Chapter 4.

Earlier it has been pointed out that initial speakers design their turns in such a way that they display the nature of the preferred response, and that recipients design their responses so as to be maximally in agreement with the prior turn. But "given evidence that a disagreement is "in the works" for some initial version of a question, they [speakers] reformulate it [the initial turn] in the direction of possible agreement, with the consequence that A) a disagreeing response is avoided, and B) the agreement that ensues makes, with the question, a contiguous pair." (Sacks 1973:16-17). For example:

(45) [Sacks 1973:15]
A. Ken you walk?
(0.4)
→ A. Ud be too hard for yuh?
B. Oh:::: darling I don't know.
Uh it's bleeding a little,

Or,

(46) [JS:11:48. From Pomerantz 1984a:77]
L. D'they have a good cook there?
(1.7)
→ L. Nothing special?
J. No. --Every-everybody takes their turns.

So when recipients potentially disagree like they signal here by withholding their responses, the initial speakers may modify the initial turn in order to establish agreement after all. As Sacks states "So the linkage of contiguity and agreement is oriented to by both questioners and answerers, can operate to avoid a disagreement, and is an aspect of a formal and anonymous apparatus for agreement/disagreement, rather than being a matter of individual preferences." (Sacks 1973:16-17).

Continuing Sacks' and Pomerantz' lines of research Davidson (1984) shows how speakers may produce subsequent versions of invitations, offers, requests, and proposals, when their recipients potentially or actually reject the initial action. This subsequent version provides a next place for a preferred response. Davidson gives the following example:

(47) [NB:31,19-20. From Davidson 1984:103]
A. Well?=I'll tell yuh.=Call information.
(1.4)
→ A. We c'n call information 'n find out.

In this fragment the initial speaker alters the initial proposal (the suggestion "Call information."), into a totally different proposal (the offer "We c'n call information"), after having learned that the recipient withholds the preferred response. This withholding is treated by the speaker as an indication of potential rejection as becomes clear when the speaker comes up with a different proposal, which may be easier to accept by the recipient.

In the next fragment the speaker extends the initial invitation by giving an argument why the recipient might accept:

(48) [NB:43, 150. From Davidson 1984:105]
C. Well yih c'n both sta:y.
(0.4)
→ C. [Got plenty a' roo:m,
B. [Oh I-

In Chapter 4 I will deal with subsequent versions of initial requests, invitations, and the like (under the general label of 'proposal'). Unlike Pomerantz and Davidson however, I will not deal with potential or actual rejection first, but with acceptance. As far as rejections are at stake they will be considered primarily as 'not-yet-acceptances'. For example, a pause following an initial proposal will not be seen necessarily as a potential rejection of the proposal. A pause may also solicit an extension of the proposal before the proposal is treated by the recipient as complete enough to accept it. If we take the last fragment, as provided by Davidson, there is no clear reason to suppose that the recipient is likely to reject the invitation. He or she may just as well be seen as withholding the response, in order to see how serious the speaker is in inviting the recipient. Especially in the case of invitations recipients have good reasons to check out first whether they are really welcome. In the case of requests for performing some action, or proposals to make an appointment for a certain date or time, a recipient may withhold his response in order to get the speaker to reformulate the initial request or proposal so that the subsequent version comes closer to the recipient's position, without the recipient needing to do any negotiation. An example is shown in the next fragment: the speaker invites the recipient to come to her party, and when the recipient withholds acceptance by giving an "Oh"-receipt (cf. 4.3.1.1), the speaker goes on to invite the recipient's boyfriend as well:

(49) [HH:TC:6:2]
H. U:::h listen, on Sunday around three o'clock,
I'm having a party here. 'Cause uh it's my
birthday this week, so if you feel like coming
you're more than welcome.
J. Oh.
→ H. And so is Jan.

It will become clear later on that when recipients withhold acceptance of a request to do something, speakers will frequently continue to explain why they make the request, after which recipients may accept the request. The frequency with which this occurs suggests that conversationalists feel that recipients have the right to know why they are asked a favour on the speaker's behalf. I will show that just as inviters should display that they are 'sincerely' inviting the recipient before the invitation is ready for acceptance, requesters should have made clear that they have good reasons to bother the recipient before the request is ready for acceptance.

Not accepting a request or some other proposal right after its delivery therefore, does not necessarily mean that the recipient is in the process of rejecting it. The recipient's withholding an immediate acceptance can also be seen as the recipient waiting to see if the speaker will have more to say to his initial action and what this may be. In 4.3 more will be said about this kind of preference organization.

4 Structure and function of remote proposal sequences

In this chapter I will present the analysis of remote proposal sequences as they occur in Dutch telephone conversations. This type of sequence is set up by a proposal for remote action (or 'remote proposal'), and usually leads to a five-part sequence. In the first section attention will be paid to three-part proposal sequences, where the first action is a proposal for immediate action (or 'immediate proposal'), in order to be able to subsequently explain the interactional function of the five-part structure of the remote proposal sequence.

4.1 Immediate proposal sequences as three-part sequences

There are two types of proposals to be distinguished: a speaker may either propose an action to be performed immediately, or at some time in the future. The first type of proposal I will call an 'immediate proposal', and the second type a 'remote proposal'.

It must be remembered that the term proposal will be used as a general term for a class of actions, all having some aspect of proposing an action to be performed by the speaker or by the recipient: requests, offers, invitations, suggestions, appointments, and the like.

A remote proposal as it occurs in telephone conversations, is for example, an invitation for dinner, a request to the recipient to perform some task, an offer to bring something to the recipient's house, or a proposal to go and swim together. Such a remote proposal has an acceptance as a preferred, and a rejection as a dispreferred response. In fact, as I will discuss in more detail later on, rejection in this case is merely a matter of non-acceptance or not-yet-acceptance of the proposal (cf. 3.4).

On the other hand immediate proposals are mainly requests such as "hold on for a minute", "let me get my diary", "let me ask my wife", or as they frequently occur in telephone conversations "Can I speak to So-and-So please?", or its indirectly formulated version "Is So-and-So there?". The proposed action is meant to be carried out immediately.

These immediate proposals set up a three-part sequence in the way discussed in Chapter 3:

1 speaker : initiative - proposal
2 recipient: response - acceptance
3 speaker : sequence closing - acknowledgement

In this section I will discuss one type of immediate proposal, a proposal made by the caller to the answerer (i.e. the person who answers the phone), to speak to the called (i.e. the person who caller wishes to speak). This happens in the following fragments in which the successive actions (proposal, acceptance and acknowledgement), are numbered as 1, 2 and 3.

(50) [HH:TC:20:2]
1 M. May I speak to Aletta please?
(0.3)
2 T. Ja:.
3 M. Okay:.
T. ALETTA:, YOUR MOTHER.

The request "May I speak to Aletta please?", is accepted with a "Ja:.", and this acceptance is acknowledged by the initial speaker saying "Okay:.". As we can hear from the recording the recipient not only accepts this request but also complies with it.

The same structure of [request] [acceptance] [acknowledgement] is found in the next fragments. Note however, that the answerers not only accept the request, but also indicate that they are about to, or are in the process of carrying out the action requested: "I'll get her for you:", "Just a minute please.", and "Hold on please.".

(51) [PtH:TC:3]
1 P. Can I speak to my mo:ther please?=
2 L. =J:a: s:u:re. I'll get her for you:.=
3 P. =Ja.

The recipient first treats the prior utterance ("Can I speak to my mo:ther please?") as a question when she says: "J:a: s:u:re.", and continues treating it as a request to bring the caller's mother to the telephone by indicating: "I'll get her for you:.". The response is acknowledged by the initial speaker: "Ja.".

Following the request then, the recipient accepts the request, and may or may not indicate the carrying out of the requested action. In other cases we find "Here she comes", or similar indications of compliance. In this way recipients demonstrate that they hear such an initial utterance like 'Is So-and-So there?', as a request to call So-and-So when present. They further demonstrate that the acceptance is not just a conversational action, but was a sincere acceptance. When recipients initially respond with a "Ja", they indicate that they intend to carry out what has been (indirectly) asked for. The factual proof of the recipient's sincerity will follow when the person called begins to speak.

Sometimes acceptance is made by an indication of the performance of the action as such, as in:

(52) [HH:TC:18:81]
    1 R. Could I speak to her?
→ 2 J. I'll call her. [One moment please.
    3 R.   [Okay. Tha:nks.

As has been discussed elsewhere (Sacks Oct.31.1967, L8; see also Levinson 1983:360-4), requests are usually preceded by a pre-request sequence. Pre-requests are used to ascertain the grounds on which the intended request may be refused. In case of requests calling someone else to the telephone, this means that callers inquire whether the person they wish to speak to is there, before requesting her or him to the telephone:

(53) [HH:TC:18:81]
→   R. Is your wife there?
       J. She's there ja:.
    1 R. Could I speak to her please?

The next two fragments show that if the inquiry is negatively answered, the request will not follow:

(54) [HH:TC:18:95]
    R. Is your mother at home?
    D. No:.
    R. Is your mother not at ho:me?

(55) [HH:TC:18:84]
    R. Is your mother at home?
    M. No. She's at the office.
    R. Is she at the office.

As Levinson (1983:361) argues, there is a preference for responding to the pre-requesting inquiry with an offer, or with the acceptance of the as-yet-unstated request. This however seems only partially to be the case. As pointed out before answerers tend to respond to a pre-request utterance in two different ways. First, they may treat it as an inquiry ("Ja"; "She's there ja:."), and next they may treat it as an as-yet-unstated request ("I'll get her for you:."; "Just a minute please."). In saying "Just a minute please.", or "One moment please.", recipients not only indicate the performance of the requested action, they also demonstrate their understanding of the inquiry as having been done in the service of an (unstated) request.

In the next fragment we find only one utterance in the second sequence-position.

(56) [HH:TC:5:13]
 1 H. Is Annet around?=
 2 G. =Ja sure.=
 3 H. =Okay.

Note that whether the answerer produces one or two responses to a pre-request (i.e. an answer to the inquiry as well as an acceptance of the request), is partly determined by the speed with which the caller acknowledges this second-positioned response. When the caller produces the "Okay" as fast as happens in this fragment, a more explicit acceptance becomes superfluous. Thus the preference Levinson refers to is primarily the outcome of how the speaker treats the response to his initial utterance. In this fragment the "Ja sure.", may mean "Yes she's in", or "Yes, I'll get her for you". And by responding to this utterance with an "Okay", the caller treats it as the acceptance of her unstated request.

What we have seen so far is that conversationalists may take the long trajectory of inquiry → answer → request → acceptance → announcement → thanking, or they may take the shortest trajectory possible of inquiry → acceptance (of unstated request) → acknowledgement.

I would like to formulate two rules of interpretation and production with respect to these specific requests calling someone else to the telephone. The rules are similar though simpler than the rules for certain types of requests provided by Labov & Fanshel (1977:78). The first rule says:

> 'If, in the opening section of a telephone conversation, the caller inquires whether some identified

> person is in, this inquiry is heard as a request to call that person to the telephone.'[1]

The second rule says:

> 'When, in the opening section of a telephone conversation, the inquiry whether some identified person is in, is answerered positively, and without further qualification [2], this is heard as the acceptance of the unstated request to call that person to the telephone'.

Rules as provided above can be formulated because of the overall organisation of types of conversation and the knowledge conversationalists have of this organisation. The fact that people know that "Is So-and-So around?", uttered in the opening-section of a telephone conversation, is meant as "please, let me speak to So-and-So", also implies that if a caller does not want anything else than just to know whether So-and-So is present, he should formulate the inquiry in such a way that it will not be taken by the recipient as a pre-request. I will give one example of such a solution. P. calls the dentist's office, and gets the assistant Bonnie.

(57) [HH:TC:21:1]
B. Bonnie speaking.
P. Ja. Good afternoon. This is Van der Broeck speaking. I planned to come by this afternoon. But I just wanted to know if you: u:h if he was in.
B. U::h we:ll he's just gone out. A:nd within an hour and a half he should be back here. So around three more or less.

By first explaining his reason for the inquiry, the caller makes it clear that the inquiry is to be heard as just a request-for-information rather than a pre-request; this is further indicated by the format of the inquiry "I just wanted to know if".

In summary this three-part proposal sequence has as its first action a proposal to carry out some action right now. The recipient accepts this proposal, perhaps by indicating that he is performing the action, and the speaker acknowledges the acceptance.

4.2 Remote proposal sequences

If one looks at Dutch telephone conversation data, it turns out that the majority of the proposals occurring are remote proposals setting up a five-part sequence. This structure is as follows:

1 speaker : remote proposal
2 recipient: acceptance
3 speaker : request-for-confirmation
4 recipient: confirmation
5 speaker : acknowledgement

I will first give some examples of this sequence, and then discuss the structure in more detail. The successive sequence-positions will again be numbered.

(58) [HH:TC:12:9/4]
1 F. But come over here, so we can
all talk about it in peace.=
2 M. =Fine.
(0.5)
3 F. Ja?=
4 M. =I'll be there in a minute.=
5 F. =O:kay.

(59) [HH:TC:18:21]
1 M. I'll tell her. That she should bring
this Fame record tomorrow.
2 L. O:kay.
3 M. Ja?
4 L. Ja.
5 M. Okay:.

(60) [HH:TC:6:13]
H. What time could I come?
1 R. Uh (.) let's say (.) around ten o'clock or so?
2 H. Ja fine.
3 R. Ja?
4 H. I'll do that.
5 R. Okay.

The first action in these fragments is a proposal to carry out an action some time after the conversation. The proposal is responded to with an acceptance. In 4.1 it turned out that in the case of immediate proposals, the sequence may then be closed off by the proposer by an acknowledgement. In case of remote proposals however, the proposer initiates a new adjacency pair: "Ja?"/response. This "Ja?" requests confirmation of the prior acceptance. When the recipient responds to it by confirming his acceptance, the proposer closes off the entire sequence with an acknowledgement-token, mainly an "Okay".

We take the last fragment for further discussion:

H. What time could I come?
1 R. Uh (.) let's say (.) around ten o'clock or so?
2 H. Ja fine.
3 R. Ja?
4 H. I'll do that.
5 R. Okay.

The sequence can be outlined as follows. In the first sequence-position we find a proposal: "Uh (.) let's say (.) around ten o'clock or so?". This proposal, a suggestion when to meet, is accepted by the recipient: "Ja fine". Here we have the first pair, a proposal-acceptance pair. The second-positioned "Ja fine" turns out to be followed by a next pair, a request-for-confirmation of the preceding acceptance, a "Ja?", which is then responded to by the solicited confirmation "I'll do that". After that the initiator closes off the entire sequence: "Okay".

The fact that this sequence consists of two adjacency pairs plus a closing-utterance, does not mean that we are dealing with two separate sequences. The five successive utterances are tightly related to one another in such a way that they constitute a single sequence. The second action pair is not a free-standing pair, as will become clear by its form. A single "Ja?" has no propositional meaning by itself, and in order to make sense it needs to refer back to some prior utterance. Since conversations are sequentially organized, "Ja" refers back to the preceding utterance, the acceptance of the proposal. So the second pair-part of the first adjacency pair sets up this third-positioned request-for-confirmation, which is itself sequentially implicative for the production of a response, the confirmation of the preceding acceptance. This third-positioned request-for-confirmation links the two adjacency pairs together [3].

The acknowledgement of the fourth-positioned confirmation-utterance closes off the sequence. Shown schematically:

position 1: remote proposal
position 2: acceptance of the proposal
position 3: request-for-confirmation of the acceptance
position 4: confirmation

position 5: acknowledgement and sequence closing

Chapter 4.3 will show that not just any formulation placed in second sequence-position will be treated by the proposer as an acceptance of the proposal. That is it is only after certain acceptance-forms that the proposer will continue with the sequence by requesting a confirmation of the acceptance.

The instances presented here constitute the clearest examples of the five-part sequence type, and can be considered as the proto-typical form to which conversationalists are oriented when a proposal is produced. And even when they turn out not to produce the sequence as a five-part sequence, it will become clear that this is the structure to which they orient.

In 4.4 the two separate adjacency pairs of the five-part sequence will be analysed in more detail. In the first pair conversationalists may negotiate the proposal, whereas in the second pair the further details and particularities of the proposed action are under discussion. It may take more than only five turns to discuss the matter at hand satisfactorily, and each of the sequence-positions may be extended before the participants proceed to the next-positioned turn.

The actual turns of the five-part sequence may be interrupted by insertion sequences or subsequences. These will be discussed in 4.4.1.

After the pairs will have been discussed separately, the entire sequence will be analysed from the perspective of participants making a deal by taking all these sequential steps. I will explain how they proceed, from making a proposal to having made an arrangement about the proposed action. 4.5.2 will demonstrate how recipients signal their reluctance to make such a deal by holding off the sequence to be developed.

4.3 Dealing with weak acceptance-forms

As argued in the preceding section, the second-positioned acceptance is sequentially implicative for the production of the request-for-confirmation, usually a "Ja?". This implies that in order to be able to request confirmation of the acceptance, the recipient needs to be heard as having accepted the proposal.

In sequences such as (58) - (60), forms like "Fine", "Ja fine", "O:kay", "No problem", or "Ja:: sure", may be called 'full acceptance-forms'. So I refer to utterances the proposer treats as forms by which the proposal has been accepted. It may be pointed out that these utterances are more than a minimal "Ja". As far as a "Ja" occurs in the acceptance utterance, it is followed by a lexical item which intensifies the "Ja", e.g., "Ja:: sure", or "Ja fine". This is similar to what Pomerantz (1984a) has found for agreements with assessments. Only upgraded second assessments (e.g. "beautifull" → "gorgeous", cf. Fr 38), turned out to be treated by the initial speaker as full agreement-forms, whereas downgraded second assessments (e.g. "beautifull" → "alright"), and same-evaluations (e.g. "beautifull" → "beautifull"), are treated as weak agreement-forms.

In 4.3.1 I will demonstrate that certain responses to proposals will not be treated as full acceptance-forms. In 4.3.2 it will be discussed how initial speakers may deal with the problem of their proposals, and not receiving full acceptance.

4.3.1 Weak acceptance-forms

In this subsection I will successively discuss "Ja"-receipts, "Oh"-receipts, (partial) repeats, and silences as responses to the proposal which are not treated by the initial speaker as full acceptances.

4.3.1.1 "Ja"-receipts

We often find a single "Ja" in the second sequence-position, a response which does not lead to a request-for-confirmation, but instead leads to an extension of the proposal. Later on it will be discussed in detail in which way the initial proposal is extended; for the time being I will refer to it as an 'extended proposal'.

I will first give a longer fragment to be discussed in detail. In this fragment the recipient recurringly responds to the request with a single "Ja", after which the requester continues talking to the request.

I will also use this fragment for making some remarks about the different intonation contours of "Ja", and the ways in which these different forms of "Ja" may be used in Dutch conversation [4].

"Ja" is a lexical item which is pronounced in many different ways. It may be pronounced with a falling, rising, or level pitch, (transcribed as "Ja.", "Ja?" and "Ja " or "Ja,"); the duration of the vowel may differ in length ("Ja", "Ja:", "Ja::"); and it may or may not be stressed ("Ja" or "J<u>a</u>"). Furthermore the "Ja" may be multiplied ("Ja ja", "Ja: ja", "Jaha:"), which consequently causes a doubled pitch, for example fall/rise, rise/fall, fall/fall, level/fall. Although there is some relation between form and function of "Ja", some equivalent forms seem to have different functions, whereas some equivalent functions may take different forms. There seems to be a very delicate interplay between the intonational features and the functions of "Ja". When, for example, the pitch becomes just a little higher, the conversational meaning of "Ja" may change from a "I heard you", to "Oh really?".

The main difference between forms of "Ja" is the "Ja" with a falling pitch (transcribed as "Ja."), with a rising pitch ("Ja?"), and with level pitch ("Ja,"). When pronounced with falling pitch, a "Ja." may function as a continuer or as an answer to a Yes/No question. The level pitched "Ja" (with either short or long duration) signals that there is more talk to come.

The fragment to be discussed below is taken from a telephone conversation between a woman (R.) and a boy (D.). D. is about nine years old which may explain the fact that the conversation proceeds in a way which is slightly troublesome.

```
(61)  [HH:TC:18:28/96]
 1      R. Hey listen, when your mother's back ho:me,
 2   →  D. Ja:.
 3      R. please tell her that I'm ca:lling ((or: I'll
 4         ca:ll)), because Marce:l u:h doesn't want to
 4         go to his judo-class tonight.
 5   →  D. Ja:?
 6      R. Would you tell that to your mother?
 7   →  D. Ja.
 8      R. But I'll call her before six.
 9   →  D. Ja.
10      R. Do tell her that please.
11      D. Ja.
12      R. Ja?
13      D. Bye::.
14      R. Okay::.
15      R. Bye: Duncan.
```

The first "Ja" in this fragment occurs in line 2 when R. is in the process of requesting D. to pass on a piece of information to his mother:

```
1       R. Hey listen, when your mother's back ho:me,
2    →  D. Ja:.
3       R. please tell her (...)
```

In producing such a "Ja:." in the course of the other speaker's utterance, D. acknowledges that he is listening and that he sees that there is more talk to come. This "Ja:." functions then as a 'continuer' (Jefferson 1981a). Dutch continuers usually take the form of "Ja", pronounced with a falling pitch, with a short (perhaps stressed) or long duration of the vowel. Sometimes the pitch is slightly rising, which is transcribed as "Ja?". Continuers may also take a double form: "Ja ja." of "Ja: ja.". By using such a double form the recipient seems to claim understanding or agreement of what is said [5].

In line 3-4 of fragment (61) R. produces a request that D. should tell his mother that Marcel does not want to go to his judo-class that night. Now it is up to D. to accept this request, and to make clear to R. that he will pass on this information to his mother. D. responds to this request with a "Ja:?":

R. Hey listen, when your mother's back ho:me,
D. Ja:.
R. please tell her that I'm ca:lling ((or:
I'll ca:ll)), because Marce:l u:h doesn't
want to go to his judo-class tonight.
→ D. Ja:?

Instead of saying something like "Okay", or "I'll tell her", D. responds to this request with a question-intoned "Ja:?". It is clear that requests cannot be properly responded to with a question-like utterance such as "Ja:?". This "Ja:?" may be translated as "(Oh) really?", or "Doesn't he?", and the utterance refers back to the information about Marcel not wanting to go to his judo-class that night, rather than to the request to pass on this information to D.'s mother. This "Ja:?" is a 'news receipt' which topicalizes the prior information (Jefferson 1984:202).

The next talk may be a further qualification of the "Ja," ("Ja, because ..."), it may intensify the "Ja," ("Ja, of course"), or it may in some way or other modify (contradict or weaken) the "Ja," ("Ja, but ..."). For example in the following fragment the "Thank goodness man." qualifies the agreement ("Ja:") of the prior "I don't understand ((that I'm getting older all the time)), but it's true.".

(62) [HH:TC:27:12]
V. It ((getting older)) just keeps on going man.
P. Thank goodness.
V. Ja, I don't understand, but it's true.
→ P. Ja:, thank goodness man.

Or in:

(63) [HH:TC:26:18]
K. Such a (.) nice lovely bike.=
→ P. =Ja::, that's really a very nice bike.

P.'s "That's really a very nice bike.", intensifies the "Ja::." with which he agrees with the prior "Such a (.) nice lovely bike."

When pronounced with a rising pitch and short or long duration, the "Ja?" may function as a news-receipt (to be translated as "Really?"). Such a "Ja?" solicits a response by the prior speaker, minimally a confirmation of the prior utterance, for example:

(64) [HH:TC:27:14]
A. Uh I Roy, he has u:::h reported sick today, because he'd been involved in an accident.=
→ I. =Is it- Ja?
A. Ja. ((reports on the accident))

Being told that someone one knows had an accident is a piece of news that one should not let pass by just like that. After the recipient seems to start asking 'Is it bad?', she stops this inquiry, and produces a news receipt-token/topicalizer: "Ja?" ('Really?', 'Has he?').

A "Ja?" may also be used as a request-for-confirmation, and then may be translated as "Alright?". In this work we will come across many instances of this "Ja?", produced after the recipient has initially accepted a proposal. A question-intoned "Ja?" may also be used as a 'Are you sure?' when there is some doubt about the prior speaker's 'sincerity', for example,

(65) [HH:TC:27:7]
K. How are things?
P. Okay, sort of.
→ K. Ja?=
P. =Ja: sort of.
(0.7)
P. Like okay. Reasonably okay.

By responding to the inquiry "How are things?" with "Okay, sort of.", the recipient displays that he may not be quite okay. (See Jefferson, 1980a, on 'trouble-premonitory responses to inquiries'.) By asking "Ja?" (rather than saying "Okay" or "Good", which would acknowledge the answer), the initial speaker displays his doubt whether his recipient is indeed okay, and he provides for a new opportunity to answer the initial question.

Let us return to the initial conversation (Fr 61) between R. and the young boy D. If R. would have heard D's response ("Ja:?") to her request as the acceptance of her request, she might have proceeded to produce a request-for-confirmation now. Instead she again requests D. to tell "that" to his mother (lines 5-7):

5 D. Ja:?
6 → R. Would you tell that to your mother?
7 D. Ja.

As Pomerantz (1984a) points out when a first pair-part of an adjacency pair is not successful in receiving the type of response it seeks (here an acceptance of the request), the initial speaker needs to find out what the recipient's trouble may be. One possible diagnosis of the trouble is that the recipient may not have understood the type of action of the prior utterance. What the initial speaker thinks may have gone wrong, is reflected in her or his first next utterance. This next utterance is at the same time a possible solution to the trouble, e.g. the initial speaker may become more explicit about the action-status of the prior utterance. This is what R. does when she says: "Would you tell that to your mother?". She thus indicates that her prior utterance was meant as a request to pass on the information given, rather than a piece of information meant for D. The request is now responded to by D. with a "Ja.". Instead of proceeding to request confirmation of the acceptance of the request, R. extends the prior turn:

7 D. Ja.
8 → R. But I'll call her before six.

It is not quite clear if this "But I'll call her before six." is meant as a piece of information to D., or as an extension of the request i.e. as further information to be passed on to D.'s mother. Apart from what it means it 'recompletes' (Jefferson 1981a:52) the initial request, that is, although the initial utterance was completed it is now retrospectively being treated by the speaker as having been incompleted, and it thus solicits a new and full acceptance:

9 R. But I'll call her before six.
10 → D. Ja.
11 R. Do tell her that please.

Again D. responds with a "Ja.", after which R. indicates

more explicitly that her prior utterance was to be treated as a request, and that a single "Ja" does not treat it as such. This last utterance by R. turns out to be the last attempt to solicit a more extended response to her successive request-utterances:

10 R. Do tell her that please.
11 D. Ja.
12 → R. Ja?

Although D. still has produced a single "Ja." only, R. now comes up with a request-for-confirmation, by which she treats D.'s "Ja." as an acceptance of the request.

As it has been pointed out earlier, a request-for-confirmation seeks a confirmation of the prior acceptance. So D. might now come up with an "Okay", or with some version of "I'll tell her". Note however that he does not say such:

12 R. Ja?
13 → D. Bye::.

Instead of confirming his acceptance, D. closes the conversation [6].

Now I will give some more extracts in which a "Ja"-receipt is followed by an extended proposal, after completion of which the recipient accepts. Until further notice I will refer to this new talk about the initial proposal as proposal' or as 1'. The initial proposal and its acceptance will be labelled as 1 and 2.

(66) [HH:TC:24:1]
1 D. But let me put it this way, .hh when I think
I feel like jobbing I'(ll phone) you.
(0.9)
→ 2 P. Ja.
(0.3)
1' D. Then u:h then I'll let you know perhaps.=
2 P. =You do that.

It is only when first speaker extends his utterance that the recipient produces a full acceptance-token: "You do that."

(67) [HH:TC:24:4]
1 P. Shall I call Lodewijk the:n?=
→ S. =Ja::.
(0.7)
1' P. And then (.) u::::h::m I'll call
you again about what we'll do.

2 S. Ja. Fi:ne.
3 P. Ja?

When P. extends his proposal, S. produces a full "Ja. Fi:ne.", after which the proposer produces a request-for-confirmation.

The next fragment is about H. renting one of the three holiday homes of S.'s. S. thinks that the one they are discussing now would be too large for "the two of you".

(68) [HH:TC:2:85]
1 S. But (.) really, if it's just the two
of you I really would I wouldn't do it.
→ H. No.
1' S. 'Cause the place is enormous.
2 H. No: but I'm not really in need of that.

When H. produces a single "No." (a "No." since the prior utterance is stated negatively), the first speaker extends the initial suggestion, after which the recipient accepts this suggestion.

It may be clear now that "Ja" is not treated by the proposer as an utterance with which the proposal has been accepted. Instead of requesting confirmation of the acceptance, the proposer extends the initial proposal by which the recipient is given a further opportunity to accept this proposal on its first next completion.

It has been discussed in section 3.4 that a proposal has, as its preferred response, an acceptance. And as Pomerantz and Sacks have demonstrated dispreferred responses are built into a 'dispreferred action-turn shape', which minimizes non-agreement with the initial utterance as far as possible. One way of starting off such a dispreferred response e.g. a rejection, is to state acceptance before rejecting the proposal. In Houtkoop-Steenstra (1980) it has been shown how "Ja", in response to an assertion may be used as a stated agreement, i.e. as the concessive turn-component followed by the adversative second component of the response turn. A "Ja" therefore, is a 'disagreement implicative' response (Pomerantz 1984a). The same holds for a "Ja" in response to a proposal.

A "Ja" may but need not turn out to be the beginning of a final rejection, i.e. it is the beginning of a possible rejection (Davidson 1984). And especially in Dutch where "Ja" is used in a variety of ways the recipient may use a "Ja" in a very ambiguous way, and may only later 'define' it more specifically as the preface of the acceptance, or of the rejection of the prior action. A "Ja" is therefore a weak agreement-form.

I will show some instances of a "Ja" as a preface of a final non-acceptance of a proposal, as well as a "Ja" as a preface of a final acceptance. When I will speak of non-acceptance rather than of rejection this is for the following reasons. First it should be pointed out that in my data it hardly ever happens that proposals are rejected. This may be so since proposals tend to be preceded by a pre-proposal, in which the potential proposer makes sure whether it will make sense to come up with the intended proposal at all. And like pre-requests, a pre-proposal may be responded to with an offer [7].

Secondly a recipient may neither accept nor reject the proposal, but postpone the response and in doing so, non-accepts the proposal. Although I have not analyzed it, the case may well be that non-accepting is preferred to rejecting a proposal. Finally there are reasons to believe that when a recipient non-accepts a proposal, the proposal sequence may be abandoned by the participants.

In the next fragment we see how a "Ja" as response given by a little girl to a request for her father to call back when he gets home is not only treated as a non-acceptance, but also as an indication that the girl may not be able to carry out the action requested at all:

```
(69) [HH:TC:12:47]
     1 M. Do tell Hans,
             (0.6)
       K. Ja.
       M. when- when he gets back, before midnight,
          he should ring me up then.
             (0.6)
 →     K. Ja.
             (0.3)
 →     M. You do know who I am, don't you?
       K. ((sighs deeply))
       M. Or don't you? Ja::. Martijn from Rotterdam.
          You've visited me once.
          ((noises))
       K. Ja.
       M. Ja?
```

When Kitty produces a single "Ja", Martijn inquires whether Kitty knows who she is talking to, and consequently whom her father should call tonight. And when it becomes clear that Kitty may not be able to pass on this piece of information correctly to her father Martijn closes the conversation without having returned to his initial request.

Summarizing this subsection these fragments have demonstrated that a "Ja" in response to a proposal is treated by the proposer as a weak acceptance-form. It may lead to a final acceptance, or to a final rejection, or non-acceptance of the proposal. But as long as the recipient has not produced anything more than just a "Ja", he has neither rejected nor accepted the proposal, and the proposer will try to find out what problem the recipient may have in producing a full acceptance. The proposer may then extend his initial talk in such a way that he provides a new opportunity for the recipient to produce a clearer response/acceptance. Presented schematically:

```
speaker  :  [proposal]
recipient:  ["Ja"-receipt]
speaker  :  [proposal']
```

Not only a "Ja" is treated as a weak acceptance-form, so some other forms of response are too. A (partial) repeat of the initial utterance as well as an "Oh", are followed by the speaker extending the proposal-utterance. This also holds for non-responses, i.e. cases in which the recipient does not respond within a certain stretch of time. I will give some examples of these three types below.

4.3.1.2 "Oh"-receipts

I will start this subsection by giving an extract in which a request is responded to with an "Oh", after which the speaker extends her initial utterance:

```
(70) [HH:TC:20:10]
     1  A. I wanted to ask if uh:m you could put
           the key you've got of my house,
              (.)
        R. Ja:.
        A. of downstai:rs,
             (0.6)
        A. in an envelope, and drop it at A:ns's.
              (.)
        A. in Heartstreet.
             (1.3)
  →  2  R. O:h.
     1' A. If it's possible.
```

After A. has completed her request it takes R. 1.3 seconds to respond. As will be discussed later on such a long pause is rejection-implicative. But rather than rejecting the request the recipient says "O:h". And the speaker 'post-completes' (Sacks 1971, Ch 4:13) [8] her request: "If it's possible.".

Heritage (1984b) has discussed the interactional function of "Oh"-receipts. He shows that in specific sequential contexts (e.g., after informings, other-initiated repairs, understanding checks), a freestanding "Oh" displays understanding of the prior talk, and treats it as having been informative to the recipient. The "Oh" is "used to propose that its producer has undergone some kind of change in his or her knowledge, information, orientation or awareness" as Heritage (1984b:299) says, and he calls such "Oh"-receipt 'information receipt', or a 'change-of-state token'.

When "Oh" is used to display the prior talk has been informative, this explains why an "Oh"-receipt cannot be taken as an acceptance of the proposal. A proposal, e.g. an invitation-utterance does not primarily 'inform' recipient that he is being invited, although it tends to take that form (e.g. "It would be nice if you came" (cf. Labov & Fanshel (1977:82) on the rule for indirect requests); it invites recipient to join the party, and it thus has as its preferred next action an acceptance rather than a display of having been informed.

In the next fragment an invitation is responded to with an "Oh.":

(71) [HH:TC:6:2]

1 H. U:::hm listen, on Sunday around three
o'clock I'm having a party here. 'Cause
uh it's my birthday this week, so if you
((in Dutch single 'you')) feel like coming
you're quite welcome.

→ 2 J. Oh.

1' H. And Jan too.

When the invitation is responded to with an "Oh.", speaker proceeds to invite recipient's boyfriend as well. In doing so the initial utterance is retrospectively treated by speaker as an incomplete invitation, which is now being completed and which is ready for acceptance.

We also find an "Oh"-receipt in response to a proposal to close down the conversation. In 4.5 I will discuss in more detail how proposal sequences play a role in the closing of the conversation. Let it suffice to say here that proposals for conversation-closing, though being immediate proposals, tend to set up a five-part structure. In the following conversation between father and son the last details of the father's visit to his son have been checked by father, and he now tries to close the conversation:

```
(72) [HH:TC:20:174]
     1 V. Well. We know enough. Then
          u::h (.) [because I've got
       R.          [s- sa-
       V. to call Margreet, y'know.
            (1.0)
       R. Ja::.
          ((some lines omitted))
     1 V. =Very quickly. Ja:. Because I've got to call
          Margreet y'know. She's waiting for it.
            (0.6)
       R. Ja:.
            (.)
→      R. O:h I [see.
       V.       [Right?
```

Instead of complying with this proposal to close the conversation, (e.g. by saying "Okay."), R. first gives a "Ja"-receipt ("Ja::."). And when his father repeats his proposal, and gives an account as well ("Because I've got to call Margreet y'know. She's waiting for it."), R. again says "Ja:.", followed by an "Oh"-receipt. This "Oh"-receipt is responded to by a further solicit from the father to accept the proposal: "Right?".

Schematically we find:

```
speaker   : [proposal]
recipient: ["Oh"-receipt]
speaker   : [proposal']
```

4.3.1.3 (Partial) repeats

In the same fashion as a "Ja"-receipt and an "Oh"-receipt, a partial or full repeat (from now on called 'repeat') of what the first speaker has said, solicits an extension of the initial turn:

```
(73) [HH:TC:20:630]
     1  B. U:::h she should call u:h (1.0)
           before u:h ten.
→    2  R. Before ten.
     1' B. I've got to leave uh at ten.
```

Just like the "Oh"-receipt a repeat deals with the uptake of the prior utterance. Jefferson (1972) discusses some subclasses of repeats. One subclass 'recognizes correctness', or 'does affirmation' of the repeated object, and it does not generate further talk with reference to the repeated object (Jefferson 1972:302).

Furthermore there are 'questioning repeats' which "have an intonation which expresses disbelief, surprize, etc. It signals a problem in the prior repeated talk and its work is to generate further talk with respect to the remedy of the problem. It provides that the one who has produced the object which is repeated is obliged to talk some more with reference to that object." (Ibid: 299). It has been suggested by Jefferson (1981a) that a questioning repeat may challenge the prior utterance, and that it is disagreement-implicative (cf. also Pomerantz 1984a, Davidson 1984).

However as both the fragment above and the next fragments show, a repeat in response to a proposal does not need to have a questioning intonation in order to generate further talk with reference to the repeated object. By repeating (part) of the prior utterance recipient displays that he has been informed. However the relevant response to a proposal is an acceptance or a rejection, and therefore, by providing an information-receipt, the recipient non-accepts the proposal.

The initial speaker may treat this repeat/information-receipt as a communication-check by affirming the correctness of recipient's hearing of the prior utterance. This becomes clear in the following fragment, which is taken from the conversation discussed earlier about the holiday-home (see Fr 68).

After having discussed the location and the qualities of the three vacant homes, the participants have by now decided which home would be suitable for H. to rent, and now they are discussing at what time of the year H. could have the home:

```
(74) [HH:TC:2:8]
       1 S. Then it would be very convenient for us
            if you came up to the seventh of July.
 -->   2 H. July.=
         S. =Ja.
```

"July", in Dutch "Juli", is often repeated in Dutch conversation since it sounds very similar to "Juni" (June). A recipient may make sure if he has heard the name of the month correctly, and the speaker may then say: "Ja, July, with an 'l'".

In this fragment such a repeat is not only affirmed ("Ja."), but the speaker also talks more with reference to her initial proposal:

(75) [HH:TC:2:85]
1 S. Then it would be very convenient for us
if you came up to the seventh of July.
2 H. July.=
S. =Ja.
→ 1' S. So to have you until.=
2 H. =Ja ja. Oh ja. Until.
1' S. And before.

The speaker goes on to reformulate part of the initial proposal: "it would be very convenient for us if you came up to the seventh of July", now becomes "So to have you until ((the seventh of July))."; the recipient responds to this extension with a "Ja ja" (to be translated as 'I see'), followed by "Oh ja. Until" ('Oh I see. Until'), as if he has come to understand now what the speaker in fact had said in her initial proposal-utterance. This response is still not an acceptance of the proposal, and now the speaker explains in the last line of the extract that 'having you until July' implies "And before". And though not shown here, now the recipient has come to say that he will discuss the entire enterprise of renting the house with his wife. Thus he neither accepts nor rejects the proposal, but postpones the response.

In the next fragment it becomes very clear that repeating the speaker's proposal is a way of providing for time to come to a decision as to how to respond to the proposal. Since this fragment will return in the next subsection where it will be discussed more extensively, I will only make a few comments on it now.

(76) [HH:TC:14:399]
1 G. Gerard.
2 M. (Ja.) Martijn speaking.=
3 M. =An appointment.
4 G. Ja.
5 1 M. Is that possible? Thursday afternoon.
6 (1.1)
7 M. Or would I be too late then?
8 → G. < Thursday afternoon? >
9 M. ° ( )awake ja. °
10 G. Are you (time) Th(h)at would make it easier.

```
11          (0.8)
12       G. .hh u:[hm.
13       M.       [You should do so as well.
14     2 G. U::::hm (2.0) [Ja that's possible.
15       M.               [(      )
16          (.)
17       G. Thursday. ((writes in diary?))
18          (1.1)
19       G. No. Hold on. ((muttering))
20     1 M. Friday would be fine too.
21 -->   G. Friday would be fine too.
22          (.)
23       G. Let me think.
24          (2.0)
25       M. That is (.) not on Friday morning, (Thursday
26          afternoon in principle I'll be        )
27     2 G. Well let's take Thursday afternoon.=
28       M. =Ja?
29       G. Ja.
```

In line 5 the speaker proposes to meet on Thursday afternoon which is, after some time, repeated by the recipient in line 8. After some 'thinking aloud' ("U:hm" in line 12; "U::::hm (2.0)" in line 14), the recipient accepts the proposal to meet on Thursday afternoon. However he then indicates that he may withdraw the acceptance (line 19), and the speaker then comes up with an alternative: "Friday would be fine too." (line 20), which is literally (except for the stress) repeated by the recipient. And after some thinking (lines 23, 24), the recipient re-accepts the proposal to meet on Thursday (line 27).

So far it has turned out that a repeat in response to a proposal is treated by the speaker as a not-yet-acceptance of the proposal. The recipient may repeat the proposal, and indicate that he needs some time to think before he can adequately respond to the proposal, and the speaker may wait for the recipient to have made up his mind. This happened in fragment 75. In other instances speakers tend to talk more to the initial proposal when this has been responded to by a repeat. Schematically:

```
speaker  : [proposal]
recipient: [(partial) repeat]
speaker  : [proposal']
```

Since the same thing happened in case of a "Ja"-receipt and an "Oh"-receipt, we may schematize as follows:

speaker : [proposal]
recipient: ["Ja"-receipt] ["Oh"-receipt]
[(partial) repeat]
speaker : [proposal']

A Dutch proverb says "Silence gives consent". This however does not seem to be true in case of a proposal as the next subsection will show.

4.3.1.4 Silences

Instead of producing an acceptance or a rejection, a recipient may respond to a proposal with no immediate forthcoming talk, i.e. with a silence. When a recipient withholds acceptance or rejection in this way, the speaker will again extend his initial proposal:

(77) [HH:TC:14:160/339]
A. An appointment.
G. Ja.
1 A. Is that possible? Thursday afternoon.
→ (1.1)
1' A. Or would I be too late then?

When the recipient withholds his response for 1.1 second, the proposer comes up with a candidate analysis of recipient's trouble to respond: Thursday afternoon may be too late.

In the next fragment we find a proposal to close down the conversation:

(78) [HH:TC:20:19]
1 A. Sorry Ron, ((yawningly:)) I'm going to brush my teeth, ((yawns loudly)) and I'm going to bed.
→ (2.1)
1' A. I'm ti:red.
→ (1.7)
1' A. Of everything. Of li:fe.
(1.8)
R. Ja. That's goo:d. 'Cause you're going on vacation next week.

Again the silence in response to the proposal sets up an extension of the proposal: "I'm ti:red.". And when this receives again no verbal response the proposer explains what makes her so tired. Only after a new long silence does the recipient respond. Note however that the recipient says "Ja. That's goo:d", after which he initiates a new topic. In fact the recipient does not accept the proposal for closing, he responds to the speaker's statement that she is tired of everything, of life. As the recipient indicates that is no problem since the speaker is going on vacation next week.

This series of silences therefore turns out to be actually disagreement-implicative responses to the proposal.

I will now provide three fragments in which such silences occur:

(79) [HH:TC:20:1]
  1 H. Could you call back in five minutes?
→ (0.8)
  1' H. She'll be there then.

Earlier in the conversation from which the next fragment is taken, the co-conversationalists tried to find a day for a dinner. Ronny proposed Tuesday or Wednesday, but Annet preferred Friday. She gave some good reasons why it should be a Friday, and in principle they finally agreed on Friday. That is, if Ronny's friend Marion will agree on Friday as well. In the closing-section of the conversation Ronny refers to this dinner-arrangement:

(80) [HH:TC:20:16]
  1 R. I'll discuss it, bu::t you may: get the
  situation that Marion wants it on We:dnesday:,
→ (1.2)
  1' R. because she wants to go to Herman.

Annet does not respond to the proposal within 1.2 of a second. Considering their previous discussion Ronny has extra reasons to hear this silence as rejection-implicative. And he goes on speaking and tries to strengthen his case by providing a reason why Marion might not want to have dinner on Wednesday: "because she wants to go to Herman.". This extension of the proposal at the same time re-solicits a response by Annet, who now accepts the proposal, i.e. she gives in: ".hh Ja:ja. We:ll Wednesday is alright with me as well.".

Taking the weak response-forms all together we can give the following scheme:

speaker : [proposal]
recipient: ["Ja"-receipt] ["Oh"-receipt]
[(partial) repeat] [silence]
speaker : [proposal']

Although the different types of weak acceptance-forms have been discussed separately here, it may have been noticed that they occur frequently in series or in combination. In (66) we found:

```
speaker  : [proposal]
           [silence]
recipient: ["Ja"-receipt]
           [silence]
speaker  : [proposal']
```

In (70):

```
speaker  : [proposal]
           [silence]
recipient: ["Oh"-receipt]
speaker  : [proposal']
```

In (72):

```
speaker  : [proposal]
recipient: [silence]
           ["Ja"-receipt]
speaker  : [proposal']
recipient: [silence]
           ["Ja"-receipt]
           [silence]
           ["Oh"-receipt]
speaker  : [prompting]
```

In (75):

```
speaker  : [proposal]
recipient: [partial repeat]
speaker  : [proposal']
recipient: ["Ja"-receipt]
           ["Oh"-receipt]
           [partial repeat]
speaker  : [proposal']
```

I will close this section by discussing an earlier fragment in which recipient is holding off a final response for some time by using several kinds of delay-devices:

(81) [HH:TC:14:399]
1 G. Gerard.
2 M. (Ja.) Martijn speaking.=
3 M. =An appointment.
4 G. Ja.
5 M. Is that possible? Thursday afternoon.
6 → (1.1)
7 M. Or would I be too late then?
8 → G. < Thursday afternoon? >
9 M. ° ( )awake ja °
10 G. Are you (time) Th(h)at would make it easier.
11 (0.8)
12 → G. .hh u:[hm.
13 M. [You should do so as well.
14 G. U::::hm (2.0) [Ja that's possible.
15 M. [( )
16 (.)
17 G. Thursday. ((writes in diary?))
18 (1.1)
19 G. No. Hold on. ((muttering))
20 M. Friday would be fine too.
21 → G. Friday would be fine too.
22 → (.)
23 → G. Let me think.
24 → (2.0)
25 M. That is (.) not on Friday morning, (Thursday
26 afternoon in principle I'll be)
27 G. Well let's take Thursday afternoon.=
28 M. =Ja?
29 G. Ja.

It is clear that the recipient is reserving time to reflect on the proposal when to meet as he explicitly makes clear: "Let me think." (line 23), and "Hold on" (line 19). Furthermore he uses other delay-devices: silences in lines 6, 14, and 24. The pause in line 24 is explained by the recipient's preceding "Let me think", which he does for 2.0 seconds. In 12 and 14 he produces a filled pause: "U:::h". Also the recipient's muttering in line 19, right after his "Hold on.", is a filled pause, and is a way to indicate that he is not yet ready to take his turn. Furthermore he repeats the two successive proposals of the speaker in lines 8 and 21.

As will be discussed in detail in the next section these delays are treated by the speaker (lines 5 and 20) as indications of potential problems on the part of the recipient.

The point in 4.3.1 has been that certain formulations in response to a proposal are treated by the proposer as weak acceptances. This holds for "Ja"-receipts, "Oh"-receipts, (partial) repeats as well as for silences. When recipients respond to a proposal with such an item, speakers tend to extend their initial proposal in one way or another. This extension may exhibit speakers' candidate diagnosis of the troubles recipients may have in accepting the proposal, and the by now more or less changed proposal may be more in agreement with the response.

In extending the proposals speakers also post-complete, or re-complete their initial turns, thus providing a new opportunity for recipients to produce a new and now full acceptance. In the next section we will see in which ways non-accepted proposals may be extended.

4.3.2 Speakers' reactions to weak acceptance-forms

In this section I will discuss some ways in which a speaker may deal with his recipient not fully accepting the proposal. Attention will be paid to three types of reactions by the speaker:

1. explaining why the proposal is being made,
2. analyzing the recipient's potential difficulty in accepting the proposal, and accounting for what that might be, and
3. re-soliciting a full acceptance.

4.3.2.1 Accounting for the proposal

When the recipient does not fully accept the proposal, the speaker mostly proceeds to explain why the proposal is being made, or why it is made this way, i.e. the speaker accounts for the proposal.

An account is "a linguistic device employed whenever an action is subjected to valuative inquiry. [It is made] by a social actor to explain unanticipated behavior or untoward behavior - whether that behavior is his own or that of others, and whether the proximate cause for the statement arises from the actor himself or from someone else." (Scott & Lyman 1968:46).

In the following fragments there is a proposal followed by a weak acceptance-form, or a silence. After this the initial speaker proceeds to give an account of why the proposal is being made. The account-utterance is arrowed in the fragments. The account is usually acknowledged by the recipient, after which the proposal is accepted.

(82) [HH:TC:20:10]

A. I wanted to ask if u:hm you could put
the key you've got of my house,
(.)
R. Ja:.
A. of downstai:rs,
(0.6)
A. in an envelope, and drop it at A:ns's,
(.)
A. in Heartstreet.
(1.3)
R. O:h.
A. If it's possible.
((some lines omitted))
→ A. .hh 'Cause Ans, she's coming to uh
stay here when we're on holiday.
(.)
R. O::h ja:. Well fi:ne.

The speaker's request to drop the key at Ans's place only receives an "O:h.". The speaker then adds to her proposal: "If it's possible.", and finds out whether it would be possible for the recipient to carry out the action requested, which indeed turns out to be the case. She finally provides the account why this request has been made: "'Cause Ans, she's coming to uh stay here when we're on holiday.". This explanation is acknowledged by R. with an "O::h ja:.", right after which he accepts the request: "Well fi:ne.".

(83) [HH:TC:20:1]

R. Is:: Ne:l around?
H. U::h could you call back in five minutes?
R. Pardon me:?=
H. =Could you call back in five minutes?
(0.8)
→ H. She'll be there then.
R. Oh ja. I: will.

The recipient accepts the proposal only on the third opportunity. First he requests a repetition of the proposal: "Pardon me:?". Since this proposal is perfectly well audible on the recording one may assume that R. will also have heard it.

When the speaker literally repeats his proposal, R. does not respond to it. Now H. gives an account why he is making this proposal: "She'll be there then.". R. then first reacts to this account: "Oh ja.", after which he accepts the proposal: "I: will.".

I would like to make a remark on this account why the recipient should call back in five minutes. Of all the instances of people calling someone else to the telephone fragment, (83) is the only one where the answerer does not freely say that the person requested is not there. When being asked if a person is in, recipients normally give responses such as "No, she's out" or "No. he's in a meeting". There seems to be a normative rule to explicitly state that the person requested is not there if this is the case. For example:

(84) [HH:TC:30:138]
K. Is doctor Van Veen in?=
→ V. =No I'm sorry. He might be on holiday.

(85) [HH:TC:18:84]
R. Is your mother at home?
→ M. No. She's at the office.

(86) [HH:TC:18:86]
R. Is your mother there?
→ J. No:. She's u:h out to deliver the local papers.

(87) [HH:TC:6:13]
H. Is the assistant in?
→ T. No she's ill.

(88) [HH:TC:31:310]
K. .hh Actually I was looking for Mister Koopman.
(0.7)
→ D. U::h he has a day off.

In the present fragment (83) however, the caller responds to the inquiry whether Nel is present with a request to call back in five minutes. R.'s hesitation to accept this request may be due to the fact that he recognized the absence of a "No she's not in"-type of response.

It may well be that this normative orientation to the accounting of a proposal is more generally present. An account often precedes a proposal (as a pre-proposal):

(89) [HH:TC:18:46]
L. Hey I got another questio:n,
R. Ja:.
→ L. U:h I've got a little problem, I've
got to do some washing,
R. Ja:.
→ L. and actually I can't leave the house,

because (.) I'm on sick-leave, (.) and I think
it's risky to (.) be out in the streets.
R. Ja:.
1 L. So I'd like to ask you if I could do my
washing at your place.

Or the account may immediately follow the proposal:

(90) [HH:TC:1:2]
1 P. I uh uh I call you right back,
→ 'cause the phone is downstairs >upstairs< and
it uh that's downstairs. We've got only one
phone and it's next to the bed and the address
is downstairs.

In most cases in which a proposal is not (fully) accepted, i.e., after the recipient has produced a "Ja"-receipt, an "Oh"-receipt, a repeat, or when he keeps silent, the proposer will then provide some kind of account for the proposal. The proposal made by A. to drop a key at Ans's, is accounted when the recipient does not accept the proposal: Ans needs the key so she can take care of Ans's cats (Fr 82):

[HH:TC:20:10]
A. [proposal]
R. [weak acceptance-form]
→ A. 'Cause Ans, she's coming to uh
stay here when we're on holiday.

The advice in fragment (68) not to rent the large house, is responded to by "No", and then is accounted for:

[HH:TC:2:85]
S. [piece of advice]
H. [weak acceptance-form]
→ S. 'Cause the place is enormous.

G.'s advice not to mind the girls who do not like C. to have a much older boyfriend (Fr 99), is responded to with a "Jha", and is then accounted for:

[PtH:TC:3.5.79]
G. [piece of advice]
C. [weak acceptance-form]
→ G. Because it really is uh (.) a
nonsense, (.) nonsense, nonsense.

In fragment (73) the advice to R. that his girlfriend should telephone "before ten", is partially repeated by

R. and then accounted for:

[HH:TC:20:630]
B. [piece of advice]
R. [weak acceptance-form]
→ B. I've got to leave at te:n.

And after several weak acceptance-forms in response to a proposal when to rent this holiday-home (Fr 75), speaker explains why this particular time would suit her best:

[HH:TC:2:85]
B. [proposal]
H. [weak acceptance form]
→ B. 'Cause otherwise we'll have a
very awkward week-in-between.

The fragments given in this subsection strengthen the assumption that proposals are preferrably accounted for in one way or another. That is, the proposer should make clear why the action is being proposed to the recipient when this is not apparent. As Scott & Lyman say, an account is not called for "when people engage in routine, common-sense behavior in a cultural environment that recognizes that behavior as such." (Scott & Lyman 1968:46-7). When the account is neither apparent nor voluntarily provided, the recipient may solicit an account by responding to the proposal with only a weak acceptance-token.

J. Wilson (1980) discusses a similar point for question-answer sequences. He says that apart from sequential constraints there are 'social communication constraints' on the production of certain utterances. "Hearers may expect to locate in a question a reason for the question, what I shall call a reason for contract.". (Wilson 1980:64). Wilson conducted an experiment, and solicited answers from his wife, friends, and colleagues in order to test the existence of a reason for contract. "Such a contract states that a speaker when using a question has a responsibility to mark that question in terms of the 'reason' for its occurrence. By 'mark' it is meant that the 'reason' for the question may be located or inferred from the structure of the question in context. Within this general definition 'marking' may take place in the surface syntax, the surrounding context, in terms of background knowledge and in discourse position." (Ibid.:65) When this 'reason' is not apparent, and not provided by the questioner, the recipient may answer the question, and then query the reason for asking when it becomes clear that this will not otherwise be supplied. For example:

Question: Do you feel alright?
Answer : Yes, sure.
Query : Why do you ask?

Or recipient may query the question immediately, for example:

Question: What age is your mother?
Query : Why?

In most instances in this experiment, recipients preferred the first option (answer + query), and Wilson presents two not necessarily mutually exclusive answers to the question why this is so: "Firstly it might be argued that the use of an immediate query in our society would be seen as rude. If such is the case, the preference for an answer before a query may be seen as the result of a politeness factor: a sociocultural constraint as opposed to a social communication constraint. A second answer to this problem (and in relation to the 'reason for contract' the most logical) is, that in terms of the reason for contract initial responsibility is placed on the questioner. The hearer, being aware of this, assumes a reason will be supplied once the answer has been given. Some evidence for this assumption may be found in cases where the answer is supplied in the first position, followed by a short pause, which can be observed after the answer and just before the query. This pause seems to be a space to be filled - the answerer in this pause gives the opportunity for the questioner to supply the reason which has not been apparent." (Ibid.:68).

If we compare Wilson's findings with respect to the way in which the reason for asking is solicited by recipients, to the way in which the reason for proposing is solicited, there seems to be a qualitative as well as a quantitative difference. Whereas recipients of questions may answer the question, and then wait for the reason, i.e. the account of the question, recipients of proposals tend to solicit the account first, and only when this is provided accept the proposal. Furthermore recipients of questions may explicitly ask for the account ("Why are you asking?"), whereas recipients of proposals seem to prefer a more indirect way of soliciting the account, i.e. by responding to the proposal by a weak acceptance-form.

The reason for this may be that generally speaking, there is more at stake for a recipient when he is asked to accept a proposal than there is when he is asked to answer a question. This then would also mean that the responsibility for the initial speaker to account for the action is stronger in the case of a proposal, i.e. a request for action than in the case of a question, i.e. a request for information.

This would mean that an 'adequate' proposal-utterance, i.e. an utterance complete enough to be treated as a proposal to be accepted, contains - either implicitly or explicitly - the account as to why it is being proposed. The account may precede the proposal or it may immediately follow it. A proposal could therefore be schematized as 'Proposal [account + proposal]'. In Houtkoop & Mazeland (1982, 1985) this type of turn-structure was discussed with respect to suggestions. Suggestions were treated as Open Discourse Units (cf. 3.2), since whether or not the account will be produced explicitly is a matter of the participants' negotiation. Recipient may wait for the account to be produced before accepting the suggestion, or he may accept the suggestion without having been given an account.

In the data provided in this subsection proposers confronted with a weak acceptance-form have diagnosed the problem as being due to the proposal not being complete enough to accept, and concluded that the missing part of the initial utterance is the account. In providing the account proposers may be seen as re-completing their initial utterance. However proposers may also assume recipients to have a different kind of trouble in accepting the proposal. This will be discussed in the following subsection.

4.3.2.2 Analyzing recipient's problem

When a recipient provides a dispreferred response to a proposal, that is, a rejection implicative weak acceptance-form, he is doing an accountable action. Rather than soliciting an account from the recipient the speaker himself may provide one. However since the speaker does not know why his recipient non-accepts the proposal, the account is a 'candidate account'. For example:

(91) [HH:TC:14:160/339]
A. An appointment.
G. Ja.
A. Is that possible? Thursday afternoon.
(1.1)
→ A. Or would I be too late then?

In this extract the speaker continues to extend his initial turn after not having received a response within 1.1 seconds of time. The speaker now indicates that the recipient may have a problem with respect to the suggested time (Thursday afternoon): "Or would I be too late then?"

In the following fragment we find again the initial speaker accounting for the possible reason why the recipient is responding with a weak acceptance-form:

(92) [HH:TC:12:47]
M. Do tell Hans,
(0.6)
K. Ja.
M. when- when he gets back, before midnight,
he should ring me up then.
(0.6)
K. Ja.
(0.3)
→ M. You do know who I am, don't you?

The speaker's candidate account why Kitty is producing a weak acceptance-form is that she may not know who the speaker is, and therefore whom her father is supposed to call that night. As we have seen earlier the speaker then provides the solution and explains who he is: Martijn from Rotterdam, the person who Kitty visited once.

In the following example we find a candidate account by the speaker less explicit than in the fragments above:

(93) [HH:TC:6:2]
H. U:::h listen, on Sunday around three
o'clock, I'm having a party here 'cause
it's my birthday this week, so if you
feel like coming you're quite welcome.
J. Oh.
→ H. And so is Jan.

In this fragment H. invites J. to attend the party. It needs to be pointed out here that H. refers to J. only, since Dutch discriminates between 'je' or 'jij', as the singular personal pronoun 'you', and 'jullie' as the plural 'you'. This invitation is responded to with a weak acceptance-form ("Oh."), after which speaker proceeds to invite J.'s boyfriend as well. This addition to the initial proposal may be seen as a repair, solicited by recipient's weak acceptance-form; rather than inviting just 'you', now 'both of you' are being invited. Since there is a strong tendency in Holland to invite couples (or 'you and your partner'), rather than inviting one, this weak acceptance-form may be seen as a display of recipient having recognized the 'poor' character of the invitation. Furthermore recipient and her friend are just "quite welcome" if they "feel like coming". It may be that such 'weak invitations' receive weak acceptances.

Proposals may consist of several parts, for example, (1) to come by (2) at seven o'clock. Or (1) to baby-sit (2) tomorrow-night (3) from eight till eleven. This means that a recipient after having heard a proposal and having acknowledged it, may wait for the still missing next part, whether or not speaker intended to come up with such a next part. So instead of treating a proposal as lacking its account, it may also be treated as only part of what should or might be proposed. For example:

```
(94) [HH:TC:15:134]
     M. I'll come by tomorrow.
          (0.9)
 →   M. Arou[nd-
     F.     [Ja no fine.
     M. Around half past five.
```

When F. initially withholds a response to the proposal, M. starts to add the precise time he will arrive. But before he has mentioned the time, the recipient accepts his proposal. Whereas the proposer treats the withholding of the response as if the initial proposal has not yet been completed, the recipient now signals that this is not what he has been waiting for: "Ja no fine.". Nevertheless the speaker does finish his "Around half past five".

In the conversation from which the next fragment has been taken, participants are discussing a bicycle-trip the two of them are going to make with a friend Lodewijk:

```
(95) [HH:TC:25]
     P. Shall I call Lodewijk the:n?=
     S. =Ja:::.
          (0.7)
 →   P. And then (.) u::::::h::m I'll call
        you again about what we'll do:.
     S. Ja. Fine.
```

If the three of them need to make an appointment, and if P. calls Lodewijk to discuss the matter, the as yet unsolved problem is how S. will get to know the result of this discussion. Will he call P. or vice versa, and who should come up with a suggestion? Considering the preference for offers over requests one might expect that either S. offers to call P., or P. offers to call S., which would mean that P. might then do a second offer right after S.'s "Ja::.". By producing this "Ja::." + (0.7) pause, S. solicits P. to extend his initial proposal-utterance. Due to the intonation of this "Ja::.", it is to be heard as a continuer by which the initial utterance is treated as an incomplete offer. In the pause following the continuer, S. nevertheless has an opportunity to 'repair' this continuer into a full acceptance, followed by offering to call P.; but S. sticks to his continuer, and next P. comes up with the second (part of his) proposal. In this way P.'s proposal is an interactionally achieved double proposal.

In the following fragment we will see again how a requester confronted with a silence, produces a next request, which is shaped as being part of the first request by means of the appositional "And":

(96) [HH:TC:31:5]
C. Could you do that as s<u>oo</u>n as possible?
(0.9)
→ C. And let me know when it's ready?
A. Ja: okay.

After C has done his initial request "Could you do that as s<u>oo</u>n as possible?" ('that' referring to the task of taking films out of a cardboard box, and putting them into a wooden box), the recipient may wonder if this is all there is to be done. And when the recipient does not respond to the request the speaker comes up with an extension of the request: "And let me know when it's ready?". Since this utterance lacks the verb and the pronoun ('could you'), it is syntactically built as a second clause of the larger proposal-utterance 'could you do X and Y?'. In this way the speaker re-completes his initial request; although the initial request was completed it is now retrospectively being treated by the speaker as having been incomplete.

We might say that in elaborating the proposal in such a way that the next proposal is retrospectively made into a next part of the initial utterance, as if this had been planned in advance, speakers treat the absence of a full acceptance as a 'legitimate' continuer rather than as a 'misfitted' (cf. Jefferson 1984) response to a completed initial proposal. That is, the initial speaker takes the responsibility of the absence of an acceptance. Later we will see that in other cases speakers treat recipient as responsible, that is, treat a weak acceptance-form as a misfitted response-form.

Before discussing this in more detail I will give some fragments in which a speaker elaborates the proposal in such a way that the elaboration adds nothing to the initial proposal. This can be seen as the speaker accounting for the recipient not having accepted the proposal.

4.3.2.3 Prompting full acceptance

Whereas the last three instances showed how a weak acceptance-form solicited a more extended and more complete proposal, the next two fragments show how a proposer may extend his initial utterance without changing or adding new information (e.g. an account), to the initial proposal:

(97) [HH:TC:20:16]
R. (Also) nice to do it ((=having dinner)) with the three of us.
A. Ja:.
→ R. Honestly speaking.

This "Honestly speaking" adds nothing to the proposal having dinner with the three of them, although it does extend the initial utterance. This extension post-completes the initial proposal, and thereby solicits a renewed response by the recipient.

In the next fragment where the speaker proposes to close the conversation, the recipient does not fully accept, that is, he does not comply with it, and the speaker reinforces her proposal and thus post-completes it:

(98) [HH:TC:20:16]
A. I'm going to bed no:w.
(.)
R. Ja:.
→ A. Must be grea:t. To go to bed.

The proposal to close down the conversation by announcing "I'm going to bed no:w.", is not complied with by recipient. Rather than saying something like "Okay, we'll talk again." (see 4.5 on conversation-closing), the recipient says "Ja:.", by which he treats the prior utterance as if it were just a remark without consequences for the continuation of the present conversation. The speaker does not account for her proposal to stop talking as she did earlier in this conversation (cf. Fr 78 "I'm tired"), she merely 'sticks' to her utterance meant as a proposal for conversation-closing, by which she gives the recipient a new opportunity to comply with.

A stronger way of soliciting a new and better response is prompting a response (Jefferson 1981a:19), e.g.:

(99) [PtH:TC: 3.5.79]
G. But don't mind these girls and stick to
   your friend and uh (.) call them names.
C. Jha.
→ G. Right?

This "Right?" does not add anything at all to either the utterance as such, or to the proposal - which has been accounted for in the prior talk. It only indicates that the response was not the right one, and that the recipient has a new opportunity to accept the piece of advice.

4.3.3 Recipients' orientation to "Ja" as a weak acceptance-form.

So far we have seen that a "Ja" as well as some other forms are treated by speakers as weak acceptance-forms. However recipients also seem to be oriented to this. There are several instances where recipients start off with a "Ja", and then add more to this minimal form. Sometimes there is a pause between the two parts. I will give some examples:

(100) [HH:TC:12:12/43]
M. Then I'll send him on to <u>you</u> straight away.
      (.)
→ F. Ja.
→   (0.4)
→ F. Very we̲ll.
M. Ja?

(101) [HH:TC:6:13]
H. What time could I come?
R. Uh (.) let's say (.) around ten o'clock or so?
→ H. Ja fine.
R. Ja?

(102) [HH:TC:30:33]
K. But would you do that?
(0.6)
→ Z. Ja:.
→ (.)
→ Z. Of course.
K. Ja?

(103) [HH:TC:31:5/238]
C. Would you do that as soon as possible?
(0.9)
C. And let me know when it's ready?
→ A. Ja: okay.
C. Ja?

When the recipient uses a "Ja" in his response-utterance treated by the speaker as the acceptance of the proposal, such a "Ja" is part of a more extensive utterance ("Ja fine"; see for other instances 4.2). In the fragments above we also find recipients saying "Ja", pausing for a moment, and then continuing to make this "Ja" into a full acceptance-form. Such a pause may be seen as a moment of negotiation with respect to the question, whether the initial speaker will have more to say to his proposal before it is ready for final response. When this is not the case the recipient may go on to turn his "Ja" into a stronger acceptance-form of which the "Ja" becomes the first turn-component.

This means that a "Ja" is a convenient vehicle when recipient wants to wait and see how the conversation will proceed. He may use it in response to a proposal in order to wait for the proposer to continue. And when the proposer turns out to be finished (because he does not go on), the recipient may use it as the beginning of a full acceptance-utterance. A "Ja" may also be used as a misfitted continuer, even though the recipient knows very well that the speaker has finished his proposal, he may come up with a continuer in order to solicit an extension (e.g. an account), or to solicit a changed version of the initial proposal which is more in agreement with what the recipient is willing to accept.

In conclusion it has been shown in 4.3 that certain responses are not treated by proposers as full acceptance-forms. Responses such as a "Ja"-receipt, an "Oh"-receipt, and a (partial) repeat of the prior utterance tend to be treated as continuers in that they set up an extension of the initial proposal. The same happens when recipients respond with a silence, i.e. when they withhold acceptance.

I discussed three ways in which a speaker may react when recipients do not respond to a proposal with a full acceptance-form. The first way was an account on the part of the speaker, explaining why he is making this proposal, or why he is making it in this way. It was argued that a speaker is expected to provide an account of the proposal, when the reason for doing the proposal is not apparent. The second way of dealing with the problem of the proposal not receiving a full acceptance, was an account of the speaker for the problem that the recipient might have in accepting the proposal. Such a problem may be that the recipient expects or wishes more to be proposed than initially has been done. Later I will discuss how recipients may thus play a role in what is finally being proposed, and consequently what they will accept. The third way was a post-completion by the speaker of his initial utterance, re-soliciting a full acceptance, or just prompting a better response.

4.4 On the double-paired structure of remote proposal sequences

In this section I will analyze separately the two adjacency pairs of which the proposal sequence consists. In 4.4.2 the proposal-acceptance pair will be considered, and in 4.4.3 the request-for-confirmation/confirmation pair.

It will be argued that in the two different pairs, two different aspects of the proposal-acceptance activity are being attended to by participants. In the first pair the proposal itself and the in-principle-acceptance, that is, the recipient's willingness to comply with what has been proposed is ascertained. When more needs to be known or discussed in order to be able to do what has been proposed, this can be arranged in the second part of the sequence. When there are indeed problems to be solved before the recipient is able to do what he has been asked to do, this occasions talk embedded in the sequence, that is, it occasions insertion sequences. Only when all the potential problems have been solved the initial speaker will close off the sequence.

In 4.4.5 I will discuss how conversationalists establish an arrangement with respect to the proposed action in the process of achieving the full sequence. Once the sequence has been closed, the initial speaker may refer to the action as a deal co-participants have made.

Before discussing the two different adjacency pairs in more detail, I will pay some attention to the notion of 'insertion sequence', as well as to the related notion 'subsequence', since these notions will be used in the following section.

4.4.1 Subsequences, insertion sequences and side sequences

Taking an adjacency pair as a sequence, where the two parts belong together in a special way, it is noticed between the two parts another sequence, an insertion sequence may occur (Sacks F' 1966, L4; Schegloff 1972). Instead of a simple question-answer sequence (Q-A sequence) for example, we then may find a QaQbAbAa-sequence:

(104) [HH:TC:12:1]

F. Hey, will you be coming too?	Question a
M. Where?	Question b
F. Here?	Answer b
M. Oh that's alright.	Answer a

The insertion sequence, the Qb-Ab sequence, is a pre-requisite for the action to be carried out in Ab-position, i.e., a pre-requisite to answer the initial question, Qa. With respect to the fragment in order to be able to answer the question "Will you be coming too?", the recipient needs to know what the speaker is referring to. When this has been made clear recipient can answer the question.

(105) [HH:TC:27:1]

M. Oh I cou::ld tomo:rro:w a:fternoon, Friday
   afternoon between starting at half past twelve.
     (0.9)
→ P. Until?
     (0.6)
M. Until around (2.6) se:ven (.) ha:lf past
   se:ve:n.
     (0.9)
P. Ja, let's do that.

Whereas the term 'insertion sequence' is a purely structural one, other authors use a more functionally oriented terminology. Thus Weijdema et al. (1982) use the term 'subsequence' in an attempt to relate speech act theory to the analysis of conversation. Subsequences are linked to "pre-conditions for successful interaction" in the following way: there are pre-conditions which must be met to make the interaction successful, and if they are not met the interaction may stagnate. These pre-conditions are formulated with respect to different aspects of the conversation: the speaker, the hearer, the utterance, the illocution, etc. Some pre-conditions are that an utterance must be audible, clear in its referents, that a speaker should be in the position to do an action (e.g. giving an order to the recipient), should do it at the correct time, etc. When a pre-condition is not met, e.g. when an utterance is not audible the co-participant may initiate a subsequence: "What?" **[9]**. For example:

(106) [Merritt 1976]
C. Do you sell key chains?
→ S. What?
C. D'you sell key chains?
S. Yes sir.

Subsequences are related to the structural notions of insertion sequence and pre-sequence, since a subsequence may be inserted into another sequence, or it may precede a sequence in order to make the production of that next sequence possible.

Although CA authors use structural notions when they talk about pre-sequences, pre-pre's, or insertion sequences, these notions in fact do have a strong functional basis. This becomes clear when Jefferson (1972) discusses so-called side-sequences. "In the course of some on-going activity (for example, a game, a discussion), there are occurrences one might feel are not "part" of that activity but which appear to be in some sense relevant. Such an occurrence constitutes a break in the activity-specifically, a "break" in contrast to a "termination"; i.e., the on-going activity will resume." (op.cit.:294). **[10]** For example:

(107) [HH:TC:31:207]
B. Would you please tell our (funny) members
of the board that I won't be: (.) able
to be there?
→ A. Well bugger me.
→ B. ((Laughs))
A. Ja. I'll tell them.

Before accepting the request recipient makes a small joke which is responded to with laughter by the initial speaker. This joke constitutes a break in the on-going request-acceptance sequence, after which the main sequence continues once more. Although Jefferson does not relate side-sequences to the notion of insertion sequence, the relationship is nevertheless clear enough. Despite the 'inserted' status of the side-sequence, it is not an insertion sequence on functional grounds. Whereas an insertion sequence has an intrinsic relationship to the sequence in which it is embedded, a side-sequence constitutes a break, and is only "in some sense" relevant.

A similar functionalism accounts for the other structurally labelled sequences. A request-preceding question is only a pre-request when it leads up to a request. This means that since conversation develops linearly a question may be a 'possible pre-request', and it only turns out to be an actual pre-request once the request has been produced, or when it is treated by recipient as a non-stated request.

It may be pointed out here that conversationalists themselves tend to indicate whether their talk is to be heard as a pre-sequence, a side-sequence, or an insertion sequence; in doing so they make use of linguistic devices and of conversationalists' knowledge of the overall organisation of conversation. I will give a few examples.

The next fragment is the opening of a call to a dentist's office, where the assistant answers the telephone:

(108) [HH:TC:21:1]
B. Bonnie speaking.
P. Jā. Good afternoon. This is Van der
Broeck speaking. I planned to come by
this afternoon. But I just wanted to
know if you: u:h if he was in.

Earlier I formulated a rule saying that if a caller inquires if someone else is present, this inquiry is treated as a request to call this person to the telephone. Given that this caller wants to know if the dentist is there without wishing to speak to him, he designs his turn in such a way that this question is not heard as a pre-request to call the dentist. Instead of producing the inquiry followed by an account of it, the caller turns the two elements around. In this way he prevents recipient from hearing the inquiry as a pre-request; instead the inquiry is presented as an action in its own right (cf. Schegloff 1980).

In the next fragment speaker M. indicates that his question is to be heard as a pre-self-invitation [11] (cf. Drew 1984 on self-invitations).

(109) [HH:TC:15:445]
M. Hey (.) listen.
B. Ja(h).
→ M. What are you up to tonight with Margreet? 'Cause I haven't seen your house at all.
B. We:ll if you wanna see it (.) we're packing tonight.
M. We:ll then I'll drop in for a short while tonight.

M.'s "What are you up to tonight with Margreet?" is defined as a pre-self-invitation when he continues to explain why he is asking this. The relationship is indicated by the "'Cause". This makes the entire turn interpretable as 'If you'll be home tonight, I'd like to come by', and this is how recipient treats it.

These two fragments suggest that conversationalists do indicate in what manner their utterances should be heard. When some utterance produced in a certain position of the conversation is normally heard as a specific type of action (e.g. "Is Annet around?" in first topic-position), one should indicate that in this case such a question is not to be heard as a pre-request, i.e. it must be marked as 'not being what you might expect it to be' in the light of sequential and other conversational features.

Insofar as speakers do not indicate whiat an utterance is a preface to, recipients rely on their everyday knowledge of the world (cf. Schank & Abelson 1977) in making inferences about what speaker may be up to. To be able to explain this I will give an extract from a conversation which I do not have on tape. One night around five o'clock the lady next-door telephoned, me and the conversation went like this:

(110) [HH:TC]
R. Do you happen to have planned to have lettuce for tonight's dinner?
H. No thanks, I still have a lot of lettuce left.
R. ((explains that she has obtained much fresh lettuce, and can not use all of it))

During this conversation I started to wonder how I was able to hear R.'s question correctly, but I then realized that if she was calling me at that time of day asking me this question it must be an offer. Why would she be interested in what I was going to have for dinner when she never calls me for such questions. Conversationalists also indicate when talk has been a side-sequence rather than an insertion sequence. The resumption of the on-going activity tends to be marked as such. A side-sequence may be closed off by topic-markers such as "but well", "but anyhow", et cetera, and the first utterance of the on-going talk may start with "But" (cf. Santjer 1985 and Cramer 1985 on topic marking in Dutch conversations).

In the following fragment recipients return to the yet unfinished five-part invitation sequence. Recipient M. and his girlfriend are invited to come to dinner which the speaker is giving for a woman who took care of his cats for a time. After having accepted the invitation, M. initiates ambiguous talk with respect to A. having invited this woman. I will arrow the beginning and the end of the side sequential talk:

(111) [HH:TC:12:74]
A. ((explains that he has invited this woman
to go out for dinner)) Maybe the four of
us could go.=
M. =Oh fine.
→ M. And she reddened deeply red behind her ears.
Mary.
(0.9)
A. Well, she isn't here now.
M. No bu:t she's now. She was. When you asked it.
A. °Hahahahaha°.
M. Mary, I- I- I- I want to ask you something very
personal.
A. [Hohohohahaha. Do you want to fuck me? Hahaha
M. [((Singing:)) Pom-pom-pom. ( )
A. I wanna ask you something personal. You wanna
make love to me? [Hahahahahahaha.
M. [Hohohohohohoho.
→ A. Well. .hh [Well anyway.
→ M. [Ah hum. Ja.
M. I think it's a good idea, (...)

Given the five-part structure of invitation sequences, M. breaks out of the sequence when he initiates this dirty joke. The joke results in collaborative laughter, which ends this embedded sequence (cf. Sacks 1978 on how jokes get laughter as the last component of the sequence). Speaker A. marks this preceding talk as being off the topic: "Well. .hh Well anyway.", which is agreed on by M. saying "Ja." The preceding "Ah hum." is often used in Dutch to indicate that something has been said or done which is out of order, or should not be done. (One may call it an 'evil-us indicating device'). The indication and agreement of the off-topicality functions as a bridge between this talk, and the return to the initial invitation sequence. Recipient re-accepts the invitation: "I think it's a good idea.".

Since this is not the place to go further into the ways conversationalists indicate whether an utterance should be heard in its own right, and if not, how it projects what type of action will follow, I will close the section by concluding that the notions of insertion sequence and pre-sequences are not as purely structural in character as they may appear to be.

Talk does not constitute a pre-sequence, or an insertion sequence only because it is embedded in an ongoing sequence. It is only a pre-sequence or an insertion sequence because it is intrinsically part of what will follow, it or of what it is embedded in.

Next I will therefore use both structural and functional terms when referring to one and the same action sequence. This means that the same utterance may either be seen as an inserted subsequence or a pre-sequential subsequence, or when there is not such a narrow subsequential relationship between utterances, as an inserted side-sequence.

4.4.2 The interactional achievement of the proposal and its acceptance

In many of the fragments shown in 4.1 the proposal was immediately followed by its acceptance, e.g.:

(112) [HH:TC:6:13]
H. What time could I come?
R. Uh (.) let's say (.) around ten o'clock or so?
→ H. Ja fine.
R. Ja?

In 4.2 it was made clear that a single "Ja" as well as a (partial) repeat, and an "Oh"-receipt was not treated by initial speaker as a full acceptance, and causes speaker to extend the proposal and thus solicit a new acceptance.

Although the main perspective of that section was to demonstrate that an utterance placed in second sequence-position must meet certain demands with respect to its formulation in order to be treated by initial speaker as an acceptance of the proposal, attention was also given to the subsequent version of the proposal. Speakers, being confronted with a continuer in response to their proposal, talk more to their initial proposal, after which recipients have a next chance to accept the proposal. It has also been pointed out that recipients are oriented to a single "Ja" being a weak acceptance-form since they turned out to add more to a "Ja", e.g. "Ja.(.) Of course". In pausing for some time after this "Ja.", a recipient may be seen to wait and see if speaker has more to add to the proposal. And if not more may be added to this "Ja." to make it retrospectively the start of a full acceptance-form. A recipient is thus able to influence the proposal that he will accept on a second occasion. And the proposal, as it has finally been produced and accepted, is an interactionally achieved proposal. Not only speaker, but also recipient has played his part in what has finally come to be proposed. This interactional achievement of the proposal will be discussed now.

The following fragments demonstrate how recipients play a role in the construction of the proposal before accepting it. In the first fragment the initial proposal to come by interactionally changes into the more precise 'coming by before six o'clock'.

(113) [HH:TC:16:160]
→ K. If I wanna have them, I'll come and get them.
(0.8)
M. What time?
K. Or are you havi:ng dinner and so?
M. I'm going to have dinner around six.
K. Ja.
(1.5)
K. °hmmmmmmmmm° Let's [see, what's the time now?
M. [A quarter to ( )
K. A quarter to six.
M. Ja.
→ K. .hh u::h well. If I wanna have them I'll come by before six.
((some lines omitted))
M. O:kay

Speaker K. initially proposes "If I wanna have them, I'll come and get them." . Earlier in the conversation it has been made clear that reference is made to 'tonight'. Since K. does not indicate exactly when he might come by that night he supposes M. to be home all evening. Rather than accepting this proposal M. asks for a qualification of the proposal: "What time?". This utterance may be seen as the initiation of an insertion sequence, or from a different point of view, as a correction solicitor or repair initiator. This repair initiator functions in the way in which weak acceptance-forms do, i.e. it makes the speaker realize there may be a problem in accepting the proposal. And K.'s candidate analysis of the problem is that M. may be having dinner. This is indeed the case: "I'm going to have dinner around six.". This new information forces M. to specify when he might come by, and he then comes up with a new proposal which is almost a copy of the initial one, except that he now adds a time to it: "If I wanna have them I'll come by before six." This renewed proposal is accepted by M.

A recipient may thus influence an initial proposal made to him or her in such a way that the speaker may finally come up with a renewed proposal which is more in line with what the recipient is able and/or willing to accept. In this way the final proposal is to be seen as an interactionally achieved proposal rather than as a proposal which is produced by one party, and accepted by the other party.

In the next fragment we find the same procedure. The proposal becomes more precise only when the recipient asks for an extension. The topic under discussion is when recipient would be able to come, and help with work on speaker's house.

(114) [HH:TC:27:1]
→ M. Oh I could tomo:rro:w-afternoo:n, Friday
afternoon between starting at half past twelve.
(0.9)
P. Until?
(0.6)
→ M. Until around (2.6) se:ven, (.) ha:lf past
se:ve:n;
(0.9)
P. Ja, let's do that.

M.'s initial proposal as to when to start the building work contains the word "between". But the utterance-part which is projected by this "between" does not follow. M. only proposes "starting at half past twelve". When M. does not fill out the projected 'until' within 0.9 seconds P. asks for it: "Until?" and M. now produces this part of his proposal. It is only when the proposal is completed that P. accepts: "Ja, let's do that.".

In the following fragment speaker gives two pieces of advice in a series ('you could do 'A' and you could do 'B'):

(115) [HH:TC:26:2]
B. You could go to the lawyer's office-hour,
(0.7)
→ B. That's tonight,
P. Ja:.

→ B. And you can call (.) uh for a telephone advice
  to the legal aid office of the Free University.
P. O:h. Would you have the number?

Although speaker uses a rising intonation-contour when producing "office-hour", suggesting that she planned to give (at least) two pieces of advice in a series, the second piece of advice is nevertheless to be seen as an interactionally generated one. The advice-giver pauses for 0.7 seconds before extending the first piece of advice, a pause which might have been used by the recipient to accept or to ask for more details (cf. Sacks, May 29, 1968:13 on 'interruption invitation' by speakers). The fact that a speaker projects two or more actions in a series does not imply that such an extended turn needs to be produced until its projected end.

A recipient may prevent a larger turn from getting completed by interrupting it, by which he indicates that the turn is complete enough for response. When speakers may only complete their utterances when their recipients will let them this implies that all utterances are interactionally achieved products (cf. Ch.Goodwin, 1979).

The next conversation makes very clear that a proposed action may be subjected to discussion before it is accepted. This conversation is preceded by an earlier one, where the participants have set a date and time to do some building work at Peter's place. Now Peter calls again to change the time.

(116) [HH:TC:27:3]
M. Martijn speaki:ng.
P. Hey hi Martijn, it's Pe:ter.
M. Hi Martijn it's Peter. U:hm ja?
1 P. U:h would it be possible for you to come
  tomorrow instead of: u:h one o'clock at:::
  around two, half past two?
  (4.5)
M. Ja: su:re.
→ M. I have to, haven't I? There's no choice, right.
  ((laughing softly))
P. We:ll, I'm just a:ski:ng.
  (0.3).
P. If you say well "mm-mm-mm."=
→ M. =Will we manage then?
P. .hh You had time till u::h what ti:me? Seven
  o'clock?
  (0.3)
M. Oh no:. I've got time till u:h ei:ght.=
P. =Ja:, then we'll manage.=

M. =>Eight o'clock<. Ja?
P. Ja.
(0.4)
M. I'll be at yours at two o'clock.
(0.6)
P. O:kay:.=
M. =Ja:?=
P. =Ja, we'll do: tha:t.=
M. =See you tomorro:w.=
P. [=By:e.
M. [=By:e.

Before accepting the request M.brings the proposal as such into discussion in two different ways. As we will see later on the first adjacency pair of the five-part sequence concerns the recipient's willingness. It may have become clear that a recipient's reluctance to accept a proposal tends to generate a subsequent proposal which is more in agreement with recipient's willingness to accept it. In this fragment we find a clear reference to this willingness-feature: "I have to, haven't I? There's no choice, right. (laughing softly)".

After the initial request there is a pause of 4.5 seconds before M. responds to the request ("Ja: su:re."). This pause is a time in which the speaker could have explained why all of a sudden he wants M. to come earlier than the time arranged in the previous call. I.e. the speaker might have accounted for the proposal now. M.'s first response to the request is an acceptance ("Ja: sure.") and he proceeds saying "I have to, haven't I? There's no choice, right.". This second utterance might be taken as a complaint that no account for the proposal has been given, not even after M. waited a long time before accepting this proposal. The utterance "I have to, haven't I? There's no choice, right?" also signals that recipient takes the speaker's initial utterance as an imperative rather than as a proposal which may be rejected, or at least may be negotiated.

Once it is made clear that the initial utterance was indeed a proposal instead of an imperative ("We:ll, I'm just a:ski:ng. (0.3) If you say well "mm-mm-mm"."), M questions the sense of the proposed action: "Will we manage then?", i.e. 'will we manage when we work from two till eight o'clock?'. And when this turns out to be alright M. re-accepts: "I'll be at yours at two o'clock."

In the next conversation the proposal to make an appointment for Thursday afternoon is discussed at length before finally being accepted. Before recipient says "Well let's take Thursday afternoon", speaker has offered an alternative possibility.

```
(117) [HH:TC:14:399]
1          G. Gerard.
2          M. (Ja.) Martijn speaking.=
3          M. =An appointment.
4          G. Ja.
5      1   M. Is that possible? Thursday afternoon.
                (1.1)
7          M. Or would I be too late then?
8          G. < Thursday afternoon? >
              ((SIDE SEQUENTIAL TALK))
14     2   G. U::::hm. (2.0) [Ja that's possible.
15         M.                [(      )
16                (.)
17         G. Thursday. ((writes in diary?))
18              (1.1)
19 →       G. No. Hold on. ((muttering))
20     1'  M. Friday would be fine too.
21         G. Friday would be fine too.
22                (.)
23         G. Let me think.
24              (2.0)
25     1'  M. That is (.) not on Friday morning,(Thursday
27            afternoon in principle I'll be              )
28     2   G. Well let's take Thursday afternoon.=
29     3   M. =Ja?
30     4   G. Ja.
```

Here we can see again that rather than one participant doing a proposal and the other one accepting or rejecting it, co-participants are negotiating the proposal. The negotiation begins in line 6 when the recipient withholds response. The speaker takes the absence of a response as an indication that his proposal may be problematic for the recipient: "Or would I be too late then?". The recipient again postpones response by partially repeating the time mentioned, and after some side-sequential talk he accepts: "Ja that's possible" (line 14), but very shortly after he rejects: "No. Hold on." (line 19), and the proposer comes up with an alternative: Friday. And while the recipient is still considering this new time the speaker qualifies his proposal as "That is (.) not on Friday morning.". Now recipient decides that his initial acceptance still stands after all: "Well let's take Thursday afternoon." (line 27). This renewed acceptance is treated by speaker as an acceptance which might be confirmed ("Ja?", line 28).

The negotiation of the proposal takes place in the

first part of the sequence before the third-positioned "Ja?" is produced. When the recipient confirms his acceptance further details of the arrangement (though not shown here), will be settled. And when all this is clear, the sequence, as well as the conversation as such, is closed.

In this section it has become clear that a proposal is negotiable by participants. Instead of having the option either to accept or to reject, the recipient may influence the action as it was initially proposed in such a way that it becomes an interactionally achieved proposal. The initiative to bring the proposal into negotiation may be taken by the speaker by treating a delayed acceptance as signifying that the recipient has a problem in accepting, and altering the proposal in such a way that it might be easier to accept it. This means that although the speaker may officially take the initiative, this initiative is co-determined by the recipient's behaviour.

If the proposal is interactionally achieved, this also holds for the acceptance. A recipient may be seen as having accepted a proposal which he himself helped to make, and which is therefore only partially speaker's proposal.

It remains to be said that when not all fragments show such negotiation it does not always mean that they are not interactionally achieved. The main difference is that in those cases recipient has not made use of the possibility to influence the proposal.

4.4.3 On the willingness and the ability to perform the proposed action

In order to have a proposed action satisfactorily carried out a recipient should be willing and able to carry it out. In this subsection it will be shown that these two conditions for performing some proposed action may become visible in the proposal sequence.

The sequence is structured in such a way that first recipient's willingness is under discussion, and only when recipient displays he is prepared to do what is proposed, may conversationalists proceed to discuss further details and particularities of the action. I will refer to this second aspect of the proposal sequence as recipient's ability to carry out the action.

These two conditions for performing the proposed action are, in one form or the other, also found in

Speech Act Theory (Searle 1969) and Discourse Analysis, which is based on Speech Act Theory.

In Speech Act Theory utterances are analyzed in terms of conditions which have to be met for the utterance in order to count as an illocutionary act of a certain type (e.g. requesting, promising, offering). Since speech acts are mainly seen as speakers' acts these conditions are formulated from the speaker's perspective. Among others are two conditions: the 'preparatory condition', which indicates what speaker implies in the performance of the act, and the 'sincerity condition', which tells us what speaker expresses in the performance of the illocutionary act (Searle 1969:71). For an utterance to count as a request the 'preparatory condition' is that speaker believes that hearer is able to do the action (Ibid.:66). The 'sincerity condition' of the act of requesting is that speaker wants hearer to do the action (Ibid.:71). Note that Searle does not mention the aspect of willingness.

Unlike Speech Act Theory, Weijdema et al. (1982) take language use as a form of interaction where both speaker and hearer are involved. Weijdema et al. formulate conditions (they use the term 'preconditions') with respect to various aspects of the interaction, the speaker, and the hearer. For example,

- In the given interactive situation speaker has the right to perform this speech act.
- Hearer is able to respond to this speech in an appropriate way.
- Hearer is willing to respond to this speech act in an appropriate way.

A different though related approach is to be found in Discourse Analysis, e.g. in the work of Labov & Fanshel (1977). Greatbatch (1985) formulates as the central tenet of Discourse Analysis that "coherence in discourse is a product of sequencing rules which, stated over speech act (or related) categories, govern the order in which such acts can properly occur. These rules are proposed to delimit well-formed sequences of interaction (coherent discourse) from ill-formed sequences of interaction (incoherent discourse) in much the same way that grammatical rules delimit well-formed from ill-formed sentences." (Greatbatch 1985:71). The accomplishment of discourse coherence is accounted for in terms of 'rules of production and interpretation', which transform utterances into acts, and 'sequencing rules' which provide for a given act following another in an orderly and coherent way.

Labov & Fanshel (1977) formulate the rule of

production and interpretation of requests as follows:

"If A addresses to B an imperative specifying an action X at a time T1, and B believes that A believes that

1a. X should be done (for a purpose Y) [need for the action]

1b. B would not do X in the absence of the request [need for the request]

2. B has the ability to do X (with an instrument Z)

3. B has the obligation to do X or is willing to do it.

4. A has the right to tell B to do X

then A is heard as making a valid request for action." (Ibid:78).

The sequencing rule says that "Requests must be acknowledged and responded to." (Ibid.:100). The recipient of a request has three basic options: (1) to "Give the response requested - that is, perform the action or give the information", (2) to "put off the request", and (3) to "refuse, with or without an accounting" (Ibid.:110-111) [12].

The analysis of the double-paired structure of proposal sequences will give empirical evidence for some of the conditions formulated by the authors mentioned above. It will be shown furthermore that conversationalists not only have such assumptions about themselves and the other party in their minds when talking to one another, but that they may also demonstrate this in the ways in which they build action sequences.

Earlier in 4.3.2.1. it has been discussed how proposals tend to be accounted for explicitly, either voluntarily or solicit, when the reason for doing the proposal is not clear by itself. This aspect of the proposal returns in Labov & Fanshel's "X should be done (for the purpose Y)".

As will be shown in greater detail in the data, first the willingness of recipient to carry out the proposal is at stake in the sequence, and secondly his ability to do it. Note however, that Labov & Fanshel have ordered these aspects the other way around. Furthermore their last subrule says that "A has the right to tell B to do X". However one would say that this should be formulated prior to the subrule which says that "B has the obligation to do X or is willing to do it", since it is a prerequisite for hearer's willingness to do the action.

It will become clear why a remote proposal sets up a five-part sequence rather than a three-part sequence. Recipients first respond to the proposal with respect to their preparedness to go along with it. Since it may turn out that they are not capable to comply after all [13], once the details of the action have become clear the recipients need to re-accept the proposal when they stay with the initial acceptance, after having learned what is really proposed. So after having 'in principle' accepted in second sequence-position, recipients re-accept in fourth sequence-position (by means of confirming the earlier acceptance), after which the speaker may close the sequence. I will first discuss the willingness to accept a proposal.

Although a proposal may be formulated as an inquiry whether recipient is capable of doing such and such ("could you do X", in Dutch "zou jij X kunnen doen"), in many cases it is formulated in such a way that recipient is asked whether he "would" do (in Dutch "willen") such and such (cf. Gibbs 1981, 1986, Ervin-Tripp 1981, Blum-Kulka & Ohlstain 1985), for example:

(118) [HH:TC:31:207] cf. fragment 107
B. Would you please tell (...)

(119) [HH:TC:18:28/96] cf. fragment 61
R. Would you te̲ll that to your mother?

(120) [HH:TC:30:33] cf. fragment 121
K. But would you do that?

When recipient accepts the proposal he may be heard as having in principle accepted, as having said that as far as he is able to decide so far, he is willing to perform the action. However a recipient having indicated that he is willing to do what he was asked, may be faced with problems or uncertainties with respect to the factual execution of the action. For example, when one is asked to call back one needs to know the telephone-number, or if one is asked to deliver a parcel somewhere one needs to know the address. This kind of detail can be discussed in the second part of the sequence. Recipient may initiate such talk right after speaker's request-for-confirmation, or he may add it to his second-positioned acceptance-turn. I will give some extracts where this occurs.

Preceding the fragment below, speaker K has explained that there is an X-ray machine to be dismantled. This is a preliminary to the request "But would you do that?", with which the fragment begins:

(121) [HH:TC:30:33]
1 K. But would you do that?
(0.6)

```
      2 Z. Ja:. (.) Course.
      3 K. Ja?
              (1.1)
  →     Z. Can it be done with a u:h (      machine).
           Or wha:t?=
        K. =I: don't kno:w. It is a Philips.
        Z. Ja.
              (2.6)
      2 Z. Ja. (I don't mind doing [that.)
      3 K.                         [Ja?
      4 Z. (          ) dismantle ja.
      5 K. Okay.
```

In the first part of the sequence Z. accepts the request. This sets up the request-for-confirmation, and instead of confirming his acceptance Z. inquires which tools are needed for dismantling this X-ray machine, an inquiry related to the factual performance of the action. So after first having expressed his willingness, he now comes to the ability-part of the action to be performed.

After this has been discussed Z. restates that he is willing to dismantle the machine. Note that this re-acceptance is treated by the speaker ("Ja?") as a second-positioned utterance rather than as a fourth-positioned confirmation. This means that after this embedded talk is finished, the participants do not simply resume the sequence at the point where they had left it, but rather they go back to the second-positioned acceptance. In re-accepting the proposal the recipient indicates that, having more knowledge about its details, he still accepts the proposal.

In the next fragment the exchange of the telephone-number is inserted in between second and third position of the sequence:

```
(122) [HH:TC:20:007-013]
      1 R. Maybe you would ask her to ca:ll me:?
              (0.3)
      2 H. Ja:. I can do that.=
  →     H  =What's your numb[er?
        R.                  [It is urgent.=
        R. =In Amsterda:m, six eight o,
           [two nine eight.
        H. [°Hold on°.
        H. Si:x.=
        R. =Eight o:,=
        H. =Six eight o:,=
        R. =Ja:. Two nine >eight<.=
        H. =Two nine >eight<.
```

(0.8)
2 H. Ja. No:. She'll be home soon.
3 R. Ja:?
4 H. Ja. Okay.=
5 R. =Thanks.=
H. =By:e.

After the recipient has accepted the request he asks for speaker's telephone-number. If his friend is to ring the speaker she needs to have his number, and if the recipient intends to carry out the requested action properly he may ask speaker to provide the number. This subsequence is placed after recipient has said that he is willing to pass on the information to his friend. And when the number has been received recipient returns to the initial topic in a marked way: "Ja. No:. She'll be home soon.", after which the sequence proceeds again.

Also in the next fragment the conversation about the details starts right after the second-positioned acceptance, and concerns the exact date and time of the party the recipient has been invited to.

(123) [HH:TC:5:13]
1 H. I would like it very much if you came
as well.
2 P. Oh that's nice.
→ P. On May the sixth?
H. Ja.
H. In the afternoon around three o'clock.
P. In the afternoon around three o'clock.
3 H. Ja::?
4 P. Ja. That's nice. I'll write it down.

When recipient has accepted the invitation and received the details she needs in order to come to the party at the right time, speaker requests confirmation of the acceptance.

Also in the next fragment we find such embedded talk concerning details.

(124) [HH:TC:15:244-5]
1 M. Would you ask him to call me?
V. To call you?
M. Ja?
2 V. O:kay.
(.)
→ V. Martij:n right?
M. Martij:n, in Rotterdam.
V. In Rotterdam.
2 V. [O:kay:.

3 M. [Ja?=
M. =Tha:nks.
B. By:e.

Note that V.'s "O:kay:", following his "In Rotterdam", overlaps with speaker's "Ja?", which means that "Ja?" does not treat this "O:kay." as a recycled acceptance.

As may now be clear conversationalists construct the sequence in such a way that there is room for taking successive steps to turn a proposal into an arrangement. In the first pair of the sequence the proposal and the in-principle acceptance are under discussion, whereas the second pair provides the opportunity to discuss further details and qualifications with respect to the factual performance of the proposed action. When there is indeed more to be said about the proposed action, this will be done before the fourth-positioned turn is produced. When this embedded talk is initiated by recipient right after his acceptance-turn, or after speaker's request-for-confirmation recipient will re-accept the proposal after this embedded talk is completed, and the sequence will proceed again from this second-positioned turn on. When, however, there is nothing else to be said about the proposal after recipient has in-principle accepted it, he or she may immediately respond to the request-for-confirmation.

It turns out then that the third-positioned "Ja?" is not simply a request-for-confirmation. It also invites recipient to discuss further details and particularities of the action. It may thus be seen as a 'last call for information' (Frankel, fc), that is, as something like: if you have any further questions or remarks put them now, and if not please confirm your initial acceptance so we can close the subject.

4.4.4 Related series of proposal sequences

In the preceding subsection it may have become clear that this five-part sequence is a unit opened by the proposal and closed off by an "Okay"-like utterance. The sequence is built up in such a way that it provides room for the discussion of the separate conditions which turns a proposal into an accepted proposal, and as will be discussed later on, it turns the proposal into an arrangement about what will be done in the future with respect to the proposed action. Whereas the base sequence is a five-part structure which may be gone through by participants quickly, i.e. filling each successive slot with one turn they may also discuss each step at greater length.

In this section I will discuss a few fragments which show that a proposal sequence trigger off a next proposal sequence, which is started before the first sequence has been closed off. This seems to happen when the next topic derives directly from the prior one, or when the two topics derive directly from the prior one, or when the topic in the course of the as yet unclosed sequence, conversationalists display this relationship. For example:

(125) [HH:TC:31:5]
1 C. .hh you can take it out of the cardboard
boxes, (.) and pack it in a wooden box.
2 A. Ja:: sure.
3 C. Ja?
4 A. Ja.
→ 1 C. >Would you do that as soon as possible<?

After having explained what needs to be done (not shown in this fragment), speaker comes up with his first proposal. This action initiates a five-part sequence. But just before speaker produces the sequence-closing utterance he makes a next proposal which is closely related to the prior one: ">Would you do that as soon as possible<?".

The following fragment shows a series of proposal sequences in which the topics discussed entail one another. Each new topic (arrowed in the fragment) is initiated before the prior sequences is closed off by initial speaker.

(126) [HH:TC:29:3]
1 M. U::hm is- could you by any chance come to
the Lingehouse tomorrow?
P. Ja that's alright.=
M. =Could you?
P. Ja sure.
→ M. U::hm does it make any difference for you?
Is- is- is would eleven thirty be fine?
(1.0)
P. U:h ja. I'll be there by then.
M. Ja?=
P. =Ja, I'll be there way before that.Ja.=
M. =Oh. Oh so you'll be there anyhow.=
((some lines omitted))
→ M. Well, shall we say (.) eleven (.) thirty?
Exactly.=

M. [=Seems best.
P. [=Seems better.
→ P. In the coffee shop.=
M. [=Ja:?
P. [=Ja:, that's fine.
→ M. Then u:h I'll really make sure that I'll be there.
→ P. And then I'll have those books wi:th me:,=
M. [=Ja?
P. [=Fine.
→ P. And u:h we'll be able to have a chat.=
M. =Ja. Okay:.
P. [Ja?
M. [Fine.
* M. I'll see you tomorrow.=
P. =See you tomorrow.=
M. =A::lright.
P. [Bye.
M. [Thanks. By:e.

In this conversation, caller M. makes a proposition to P. to meet at the Lingehouse the next day. This proposal receives an acceptance which P. requests M. to confirm. After the confirmation and before this sequence is closed off, initial proposer comes up with a next proposal: "U::hm does it make any difference for you? Is- is- is- would eleven thirty be fine?". It will be clear that making an appointment to meet "tomorrow" in a large building is too global, and it is to be expected that "tomorrow" will be specified further. This next proposal ("eleven thirty") is also accepted. Recipient's response to the request to confirm the acceptance ("Ja, I'll be there way before that. Ja.") initiates some further talk, and after a while M. returns to this prior proposal: "Well, shall we say (.) eleven (.) thirty? Exactly.". This proposal is accepted again, and the sequence develops to fourth-positioned confirmation of the acceptance. Now M. comes up with a promise: "Then u:h I'll really make sure that I'll be there.". And in response to this, P. also makes a promise: "And then I'll have those books wi:th me:,". And again before the sequence is closed off, P. initiates a new topic and sequence: "And u:h we'll be able to have a chat.". This topic is a typically last topic since it postpones the present conversation to a next occasion, so that it also functions as a proposal to close off the present conversation (see 4.5.1). This proposal then turns into the actually closing of the conversation.

The next fragment is an entire conversation between Irene and her dentist's assistant. Irene calls to make an appointment for herself and when this is settled she tries to make an appointment for her boyfriend as well.

(127) [HH:TC:29:280-296]

```
      I. Good mo:rning.
      D. Good morning.
      I. Uh-[
      D.    [Ed van Werkvo:ge:l.
      I. Ja. Irene Bank speaking.
    1 I. I would like to make a:n appointment
         with (doctor )
      D. That's alright.
 →    D. At what time would you like to come?
      I. U:::h (          ) is there any time left for
         today?
      D. Sure.
      I. Ja?
      D. Ja.
      D. Eleven thirty?
      I. Fi:ne.=
      D. =O[kay.
 →    I.   [And (.) my boyfriend would like to come
         too.=
      D. =And your boyfriend too?
      I. Ja:.=
 →    D. =Well, he can come at twelve. Is that alright
         with you?=
      I. =Ja. Fi:ne.=
      D. =Alright then.=
 →    D. =What's his name?
      I. U::h Irene and Peter.
      D. Hahahahaha. You had to t(h)hink for a w(h)hile.
             (.)
      D. Ire:ne, haha.
             (.)
      D. What his name was.
      I. (I thought this time I'd have) the right one.
      D. Hahahaha[ha.
      I.         [Haha.=
 →    D. =Ja. Haha. Okay. You'll bring Peter along with
         you?
      I. Ja. [Fi::ne.
      D.     [See you late:r. Solong.
      I. [By:e.
      D. [By:e.
```

In this conversation we find the same procedure. First there is a request for an appointment with the dentist, and when this is accepted the dentist's assistant initiates the next move into the further making of the appointment: "At what time would you like to come?". This question is answered by the patient's proposal: "U::h (   ) is there any time left for today?". This proposal is also accepted and before the sequence is closed off the assistant comes up with the next proposal: "Eleven thirty?". Right after the patient accepts this, the assistant closes the sequence with an "Okay." However after the start of, and in overlap with, this sequence-closing object the patient initiates a new, though related request: her boyfriend would like to come as well. And the assistant accepts this request by implication, while making a next proposal: Would twelve o'clock be alright?. When this has been accepted the assistent asks for the boyfriend's name, and after some further talk the conversation comes to a close.

4.4.5 Establishing agreement

After having discussed how this sequence provides room for discussing the proposal in enough detail to allow the proposed action to be performed satisfactorily, I will now discuss this sequence from a slightly different perspective. The sequence will be analyzed as a process participants go through when they turn an initial proposal into a final arrangement about the action. As the participants tend to indicate in the closing section of the conversation, they consider themselves as having made a deal. For example recipient will come to the party on Sunday around three o'clock, given references such as "Well, see you on Sunday then.", could be such a deal.

The initial proposal and its initial acceptance do not yet form a fully fledged arrangement right away. Whereas the second-positioned acceptance utterance is formulated as "Ja okay", "Ja sure", etc., the fourth-positioned re-acceptance utterance is frequently fu- lated in such a fashion that recipient seems to be making a further move towards an arrangement, e.g. "I'll be there tomorrow".

Before discussing this in more detail I would like to recall the distinction made earlier between the two types of proposals, remote proposal versus immediate proposal, such as:

(128) [FK:I:1]
A. Is Karen there?
B. Yeah. Just a minute please.=
A. =Mhm.

(14.2)
K. Hello?

The initial speaker requests recipient to do something immediately, i.e. to call Karen to the telephone. Recipient not only accepts this request she also carries it out right away, and thus speaker obtains 'proof' of recipient's reliability as regards the acceptance of the request.

Requests are not just conversational objects to respond to with an acceptance, but in accepting the proposal recipient commits himself to performing the proposed action. In the fragment above this commitment is proved by recipient in that he did indeed ask Karen to come to the phone.

In the case of remote proposals however, recipients are not able to prove their commitment right away. All they can do for the time being is accept the proposal, i.e. claim that they will do what has been proposed to them, and show this commitment as far as possible.

Earlier I referred to the distinction between claiming (or stating) agreement with a prior assertion, versus showing (or demonstrating) such agreement. Instead of stating that one agrees with what co-participant has just said, one may formulate the response-utterance in such a way that the agreement is implied, for example:

(129) [NB:1.6.-2; From Pomerantz 1984a:60]
A. ...Well, anyway, ihs-ihs not too co:ld,
→ L. Oh it's warm...

In providing a stronger qualification of the temperature ("It's warm" rather than "not too co:ld"), second speaker demonstrates her agreement with the prior assertion.

This distinction between stating and demonstrating also holds for the understanding of prior talk (Sacks, F'1971,L3:10-11). A good example is to be found in the next extract where the recipient (a young girl) demonstrates that she has understood the piece of advice she has been given, viz. that there is no problem in seeing a much older boyfriend:

(130) [PtH:3.5.79]
G. But don't mind these girls and stick to your friend and uh (.) call them names.
claim C. Jha.
G. Right?
claim C. [Ja.
G. [Because it really is uh (.) a nonsense (.) nonsense nonsense.

demo. C. Ja. So I can just go on with him?
G. Ja sure.

In summarizing the piece of advice speaker has given her (note that the summary begins with "So."), the recipient demonstrates her understanding of it. This understanding turns out to be correct as the advice-giver confirms: "Ja sure."

In the five-part sequences under discussion recipients tend to produce acceptance-formulations by which they display their commitment to do what they have been asked, i.e. with which they demonstrate their acceptance. In these fragments both the acceptance-utterances (i.e. the claimed and the demonstrated acceptance) will be arrowed:

(131) [HH:TC:12:9/4]
F. But come over here, so we can
all talk about it in peace.=
→ M. =Fine.
(0.5)
F. Ja?=
→ M. =I'll be there in a minute.=
F. =Okay. See you then.=
M. =Good lu:ck.

M. first accepts the proposal with a "Fine, and after having been requested to confirm the acceptance he formulates this confirmation as "I'll be there in a minute.". In using such an 'optimistic projection' (Jefferson 1980b) that he will come over "in a minute" he makes his acceptance of the proposal convincingly, i.e there should be no doubt that he will shortly arrive at speaker's. The recipient seems to take an active position in the matter discussed when he says "I'll be there in a minute". Such a statement displays more activity than just accepting what somebody else proposes - it is a promise to come over rather than an acceptance of the proposal to come over. Later on we will see that such an 'active' acceptance may turn into an offer to do what has been initially proposed. Furthermore note that F. reacts to this re-acceptance with a "See you then.". In fact this is a poor translation of the Dutch "Tot zo.". While "tot" means "till", the "zo" is usually used to refer to a near future, e.g. "in a minute". It is this very same "zo", which M. does in fact use in his fourth-positioned utterance which has been translated here as "in a minute". Now in saying "Tot zo", F. demonstrates his uptake of M.'s re-acceptance utterance as a promise to come over "zo"/"in a minute". F. treats the prior discussion as the two of them as now having made an arrangement about the proposed action.

I will now present some fragments where the speaker invites friends to come to his birthday party to be held on Sunday at around three o'clock. The inviter first mentions the party, and then invites the recipient to come.

(132) [HH:TC:5:458]
H. I would like it very much if you would come as well.
→ K. Oh that's nice.
K. On May the sixth?
H. Ja. In the afternoon around three o'clock.
K. In the afternoon around three o'clock.
H. Ja::?
→ K. Ja. I like that. I'll write it down.
→ K. H-a-r-r-i-e-t b-i-r-t-h-d-a-y.

In this extract recipient demonstrates his commitment to the accepted invitation in a different way. He not only states that he will write it down in his diary, he also displays that he is doing so through his spelling it out. In writing it down, he indicates that he does not intend to miss the party. This strengthens the prior "Oh that's nice" as a sincerely meant assertion. Of course writing it down does not prove one's sincerity, but it is about the most a recipient can do to convince speaker for the time being.

We might also consider other utterances by the recipient from this perspective. When recipient initiates talk about the exact date of the party although speaker has already made that clear enough, such an 'inquiry' may also be heard as a display of the importance of knowing exactly when the party will take place. [14]

In the next fragment we find recipient using the same kind of demonstration though less strong, of how she would indeed like to come to the party.

(133) [HH:TC:5:483]
H. ((invitation))
→ A. O:h how nice.
H. I think so too.
A. Ja:.
H. Will you be coming too?
A. Ja:.
H. Very nice.
A. Sunday.
H. Sunday right.
→ A. I'll write it down right away.

Note that recipient mentions the day of the party "Sunday", so she may be looked upon as making sure that she is not mistaken. Furthermore she also says that she will write it down, and she will do so "right away". Writing something down straightaway diminishes the chance to forget as we all know. And this is what recipient may also be referring to.

So far we have seen that recipients, when accepting a proposal, tend to proceed from a stated acceptance in second position to a demonstrated acceptance in fourth position, from a "Ja okay" to a "I'll be there in a minute", or "I'll write it down right away". It now turns out that participants have made an arrangement, as they display in the closing section of the conversation. The next fragment is the closing section of the conversation of which the prior fragment is a part:

(134) [HH:TC:5:483] (continuation of 133)
      H. Hey listen. I'm going to call
         some other people.
      A. Ja:.
→   H. Then I'll see you on Sunday.
      A. Ja.
      H. Ja?
      A. Ja: [okay.
      H.   [Around three o'clock.
→   A. Ja, I've written it down.
      H. O::kay.

A.'s earlier response to the invitation is now treated by H. as a convincing acceptance which she shows by saying "Then I'll see you on Sunday". And A. confirms this: "Ja, I've written it down.". So conversationalists have made an arrangement with respect to A. coming to the party. The other conversations in which H. invites people to her party also show references to this arrangement-like character of the preceding invitation sequence. For example, the invitation in fragment (132) returns towards the end as:

(135) [HH:TC:5:458] (continuation of 132)
→   H. Well then Kees. I'll see you on Sunday.
      K. Ja okay Harriet.

Whereas these invitations have been convincingly accepted, and the inviter refers to the arrangement the two have made, in the following fragment things proceed differently:

(136) [HH:TC:6:2]
H. U:::h listen, on Sunday around three o'clock, I'm having a party here. 'Cause uh it's my birthday this week, so if you feel like coming you're quite welcome.
→ J. Oh.
H. And Jan too.
J. Well thank you very much.
H. Ja?
J. [Around three.
H. [Suit yourself.
H. Ja.
→ J. I'll bear it in mind.
H. Sunday around three, right?

Whereas the other invitation-recipients responded to the invitation with "How nice" etc., this recipient says "Oh.". And when the inviter then continues to invite J.'s boyfriend as well, J. says "Well thank you very much". This is a rather formal and unenthusiastic way to respond to an invitation. Furthermore it is striking that, whereas the other invited parties say that they will make a note of the party, J. does not; she will just bear it in mind [15].

The arrangement-like character of a completed proposal sequence also becomes clear in the next fragment. Co-participants have talked about the stucco-worker coming first to M.'s and right after that to F.'s house on Friday morning. This means that F. should be home then to show the man in:

(137) [HH:TC:12:13]
M. You'd have to show him in on Friday morning then.
F. A::h no problem man.
M. No problem?
F. No:ho:. No problem at all.=
→ M. =I'll call him right now.
F. Okay.
M. Good lu:ck.

Recipient moves from a second-positioned "A:h no problem man." to the stronger fourth-positioned "No:ho:. No problem at all". This is followed by speaker displaying that the participants have made an arrangement which makes it possible to telephone the stucco-worker, and tell him what to do.

In the next and last fragment co-participants have made an arrangement for Saturday around eleven o'clock, as speaker displays in his sequence-closing utterance:

"I'll be seeing you then.":

(138) [HH:TC:15:298]
M. Listen Klaas, shall we say Saturday
around eleven o'clock?
K. (Fine)
M. Hja?
K. Okay.
→ M. I'll be seeing you then.
K. Alright then.=
M. [=Good lu:ck.
K. [=Okay.
M. Bye:bye:.

Earlier I referred to the second adjacency pair as a request-for-confirmation/confirmation sequence. Later it was pointed out that this request looks not only for a confirmation of the prior acceptance, it also provides room for discussing further details of the proposed action.

As has now become clear there is even more going on here. Recipient responds to this request with a turn-format which displays commitment to his acceptance rather than simply recycling his prior acceptance of the proposal. By going through this process of proposing → accepting → showing commitment, the initial proposal turns into an arrangement which can be accounted for in case the recipient should not after all perform the action. And when initial speaker acknowledges the fourth-positioned utterance with an "Okay.", this may be heard as an acknowledgement of the proposal having now become an arrangement.

In this subsection I sometimes referred to the re-acceptance utterance as a 'promise'or 'offer'. I will now show how this fourth-positioned utterance may indeed be treated by participants as recipient's offer to carry out the action just discussed and accepted. In treating recipient's re-acceptance utterance as an offer, this utterance becomes even stronger than a demonstration of recipient's commitment to the action. I will first give an example of this procedure.

(139) [HH:TC:27:3]
F. U:h would it be possible for you to
come tomorrow instead of: u:h one o'
clock at::: around two, half p<u>a</u>st two?
(4.5)
M. Ja: su:re.
((embedded talk omitted))
→ M. I'll be at your place at tw<u>o</u> o'cl<u>o</u>ck.

(0.6)
F. O:kay:.=
M. =Ja:?=
F. =Ja, we'll do: tha:t.=
M. =See you tomorro:w.

The arrowed utterance of the recipient functions as a pivot. It is a fourth-positioned re-acceptance after which speaker produces a fifth-positioned sequence-closing "O:kay:.". This "O:kay:.", however turns out to not close the topic under discussion. M. now produces a "Ja:?", a form used for requesting confirmation of the prior acceptance. And initial speaker responds to this "Ja:?" with "Ja, we'll do: tha:t.".

This means that in treating initial speaker's fifth-positioned "O:kay:" as an utterance to be confirmed, M. treats it as an acceptance of his own "I'll be at your place at two o'clock.", which thus becomes an initiative retrospectively, an offer rather than a response, i.e. an acceptance. In this way initial recipient switches roles; from initially having been the recipient of a proposal, i.e. request, he now defines himself as the initiator of a proposal, i.e. an offer, a change of roles with which his co-participant agrees.

The sequence may be seen as being mirrored, in which process the fourth-positioned turn functions as the pivotal point:

1 proposal
2 acceptance
3 request-for-confirmation
4 confirmation = 1 offer
2 acceptance
3 request-for-confirmation
4 confirmation
5 sequence closing

In promising to perform the action he was initially requested to perform, after having accepted the request to carry out this very same action, initial recipient seems to do all he can in order to be convincing. This process also occurs in the next fragment, where the "he" refers to the stucco-worker, who will first work at M.'s, and then will be sent over to F.'s.

(140) [HH:TC:12:12]
M. The:n u:h I can send him over to you?
F. Ja of course.
(0.7)
M. Okay.

→ F. Of course. The:n I'll make sure I'll settle it.
(0.6)
M. Oh fine.
F. Ja?

After recipient's acceptance we get an "Okay", which recipient treats as a regular request-for-confirmation when he produces a re-acceptance utterance. This utterance is followed by an utterance, which is then turned into an offer. Rather than saying "Okay", initial speaker produces an utterance which may be seen as an acceptance. And this is how initial recipient treats it when he reacts to it with a "Ja?".

Again the initial recipient turns the sequence around, and consequently switches the conversational roles, and after having accepted the proposal he offers now to "settle it".

In conclusion we may say that in the course of this chapter the ways in which recipients display their sincerity with respect to their acceptance of the action proposed to them, have become stronger and more intense. While the initial response utterance may be a rather straightforward acceptance, the re-acceptance utterance tends to be stronger. Recipients may upgrade their initial utterance to the extent that they seem to take a rather active part in the discussion; they may act as if they were on their way to carry out the task. This re-acceptance utterance may take the form of an offer ("I'll do that"), and it may become even stronger when the utterance does indeed turn out to be sequentially treated as an offer when both the sequence and the initial conversational roles are switched. One party, having started off as the proposer of some action, ends up as the recipient of an offer to perform this action.

Apart from that it has been shown that recipients may say things which suggest that they really want to do what has been proposed. If they are supposed to call back they may make sure that they have the right number, and if they do not have speaker's telephone-number they may ask for it. And if they are invited to a party they may repeat the exact time of the party, and so show that they really want to come.

These are all moves by which recipients display the conviction with which they are accepting the initial proposal. Through them recipients indicate to speaker that they can be relied upon to do what was asked, to act on this acceptance - hence that their acceptance is not merely a number of polite words, an empty agreement, but one which they will fulfill.

4.5 Proposal sequences as conversation-closing implicative sequences

There are many instances of proposals which start off as a five-part sequence without being entirely realized as such. In this section I will show that such instances are not 'counterexamples'; they are not three- (or four-) part sequences as they may seem to be, but fore-shortened or unfinished five-part sequences. The five-part sequences as they have been discussed so far, occur frequently at the end of the conversations, i.e. they often precede the closing of the conversation. What is more they often seem to play an essential part in the accomplishment of bringing the conversation to a close. To make this point clear I will discuss some of the literature on conversation-closing in 4.5.1.

The role these sequences play in the accomplishment of the conversation-closing will be used as an explanation for the fact that many of the sequences are not worked through in their entirety by the participants. These 'unfinished sequences' will be discussed in 4.5.2.

4.5.1 Opening up closing by a proposal sequence

In their paper "Opening Up Closings", Schegloff & Sacks (1973) describe the ways in which conversationalists solve the problem "how to organize the simultaneous arrival of the co-conversationalists at a point where one speaker's completion will not occasion another speaker's talk, and that will not be heard as some speaker's silence." (op.cit.:237). There are utterances like "We:ll" and "Okay" which, when placed at the analysable end of a topic, operate as 'possible pre-closings' (Ibid.: 247), i.e. as proposals [16] to close the conversation.

They are called 'possible' pre-closings because they do not need to be treated as pre-closings. "One feature of their operation is that they occupy the floor for a speaker's turn without using it to produce either a topically coherent utterance or the initiation of a new topic. With them a speaker takes a turn whose business seems to be to 'pass', i.e. to indicate that he has not now anything more or new to say, and also to give a 'free' turn to a next who, in that such an utterance can be treated as having broken with any prior topic, can without violating topical coherence take the occasion to introduce a new topic, e.g., some heretofore unmentioned mentionable. After such a possible pre-closing is specifically a place for a new topic beginnings." (op.cit.:246).

When the "Okay" is responded to by another "Okay", "these two utterances constitute not a possible, but an actual first exchange of the closing section. The pre-closing ceases to be 'pre'- if accepted, for the acceptance establishes the warrant for undertaking a closing of the conversation at some 'here'." (Ibid.:248). When an "Okay" has been accepted as a pre-closing by being responded to with a second "Okay", the conversation may be terminated, as is illustrated below in an 'archetype closing' (the term as well as the example are from Button, fc).

(141) [Campbell:7:12, simplified]
Annie: And I won't forget,
Mac : ('Kay),
Annie: Okay,
Mac : Bah
Annie: Bye:,

Closing sections may be more extended than the one above. Schegloff & Sacks say that "Among others, closings may include 'making arrangements', with varieties such as giving directions, arranging later meetings, and the like; re-invocation of certain sorts of materials talked of earlier in the conversation, in particular, re-invocations of earlier made arrangements (for example, 'See you Wednesday') and re-invocations of the reason for initiating the conversation (for example, 'Well, I just wanted to find out how Bob was') (...) and components that seem to give a 'signature' of sorts to the type of conversation, using the closing section as a place where recognition of the type of conversation can be displayed (for example, 'Thank you'). Collections of these and other components can be combined to yield extended closing sections." (Schegloff & Sacks 1973:256).

It becomes clear from looking at telephone conversations, that closing down a conversation is a process where these topic-types serve a crucial function. Just as conversationalists, especially when they are acquaintances or friends, tend to do some extended work to open the conversation and to arrive at the reason-for-calling, they seem to close the conversation gradually. In this process the making of an arrangement is a crucial topic-type since it moves the present conversation up to a later moment in the future (cf. Button fc). I should like to say something more about this here. It may be noted that there are other references to a shared future in this closing section: "Well, see you", "See you soon", "See you Sunday", et cetera. Such a reference to a shared future may be seen as an elegant solution to the potentially face-threatening act of closing the conversation. Conversational closing thus merely becomes a 'closing-for-the-time-being' and a postponement of the interaction to a next occasion. Phrased differently, it only closes the present conversation, not the broader interaction.

Making arrangements may be seen as part of this reference to a shared future, and it makes a "see you soon" a sequentially appropriate next action. If one looks at doctor-patient interaction, one may notice that doctors seem to use this closing-implicative topic-type as well [17]. In the next fragment the doctor (D.) has prescribed medicines and now comes up with:

```
(142) [HA:AP:122]
      D. And then I would like you to, when you've
         finished your cure, (0.7) that you get in
         touch with me, whatever happens, (...)
      P. Ja ja (   )=
      D. =J[a?
      P.   [Thank you, in [any case.
      D.                  [That's a deal then,=
      P. =(Bye)
             (.)
      D. Bye bye.
```

Also psychotherapists make use of a reference to a next meeting as a closing-implicative topic-type; their last topic tends to indicate what might be discussed in the next therapy-session. In this type of interaction, however, it also serves a special therapeutic function in that the present session needs to be closed down carefully in order not to upset the client, or to provide time for the client to calm his emotions or to stop crying [18].

References to the recipient's future only seem to be used as a closing implicative device in televised 'chat-shows'. When having a conversation with, for example, a film star, the interviewer may inquire about her or his next film, and when this has been answered he may say "I wish you good luck".

Making arrangements and referring to the next meeting is a strong closing-device, since by transferring the present conversation to a next occasion one gradually moves out of this conversation. Making arrangements therefore should not be seen as a preface to closing, but rather as part of the closing section. This does not only hold for making arrangements on a shared future activity, but also holds for other types of arrangements, such as arranging for one of the conversationalists to perform some action, e.g. calling somebody else. Whatever the type of arrangement conversationalists are involved in, it always implies a future activity. And in referring to this future participants are moving out of the present activity of conversing. Seen in this way making an arrangement constitutes a last topic, making further closing sequentially relevant.

With respect to this something needs to be said about the topical organization of conversation. A conversation may consist of a series of topics, or 'mentionables' (Schegloff & Sacks 1973:242). The topical section of the conversation has a position for a 'first topic'; this is not a first topic of a series of topics, but rather the (claimed) 'reason-for-calling' ("I'm calling because..."). The reason-for-calling may be preserved through the conversation, and may be referred to again for purposes of closing down the topical section.

There are other topic-types such as making arrangements, which are typically 'last topics' after which the conversation may be closed down.

The conversation may be monotopical, in which case the first topic is also the last topic. When a caller mentions a reason-for-calling without signalling that there are more topics to come, the conversation may be considered to be 'in principle' monotopical. That is, there may be more topics to follow initiated by either caller or answerer, but this has not been signalled as yet.

Earlier in this chapter it has been made clear that proposal sequences result in the co-participants having made an arrangement about the proposed action. In the fragments to be found below it will be seen that the last-positioned "Okay"-like utterance of the proposal sequence not only closes this sequence, but is simultaneously treated by the next speaker as a possible pre-closing object, i.e. this "Okay" will be responded to by a second "Okay", which accepts the prior "Okay" as a pre-closing proposal.

The first fragment is preceded by R's request to the person called to call the recipient's mother to the telephone. However the mother turns out not to be at home.

```
(143) [HH:TC:18:88]
      R. Well, listen,
      K. Ja.
      R. do tell her (...) ((that she)) must
         call me before Friday.
      K. Ja:.
      R. Just to make an appointment.
      K. Okay.
      R. Ja:?=
      K. =Ja.=
→     R. =Okay:.=
→     K. =Ok[ay.
→     R.    [Well, see you uh?=
      K. =By[e:.
      R.    [Bye.
```

In a call to the dentist, we find:

```
(144) [HH:TC:6:22]
      H. What time could I come?
      R. Uh (.) let's say (.) around ten o'clock or so?
      H. Ja fine.
      R. Ja?
      H. I'll do that.
→     R. Ok[ay.
→     H.   [Okay. Thanks a lot.
      R. [By:e.
      H. [By:e.
```

In the next fragment the recipient of the proposal has received the telephone number he needs in order to be able to call someone, and he then returns to the main sequence:

```
(145) [HH:TC:15:214]
      H. Two five three.
             (.)
      H. I'll just give him a call.
→     M. O:kay.
→     H. Okay.Thanks.
      M. Bye bye.
```

The five-part proposal sequence shades off into further closing of the conversation in that the fifth-positioned "Okay", not only closes the proposal sequence, but it is also treated by the recipient as a proposal for conversation-closing since he responds to this "Okay" with a second "Okay". The fifth-positioned "Okay" thus has served a double conversational function - it is a last-positioned sequence-closing object as well as a first-positioned pre-closing object.

Schematically:

1 remote proposal
2 acceptance
3 request-for-confirmation
4 confirmation
5 sequence closing ("Okay") = 1 pre-closing ("Okay")
                                                2 acceptance ("Okay")

The occurrence of the two "Okay's" is in keeping with Schegloff & Sacks' observation. However such an "Okay"-exchange is rarely found in Dutch materials. Instead, an "Okay" may be followed by a thanking-utterance (cf. Button, fc, on appreciations in second turns as a variety of closing-types), after which the closing-process will go on. We find this in the next fragment, which starts off with M. repeating the last part of the telephone-number he has just been given.

(146) [HH:TC:15:198]
M. Two three eight.
B. Ja. That's correct.
M. I u:h try to get in touch with them.
B. Very nice.
→ M. Okay:.
→ B. Thanks.
(.)
B. By:e.

It will have been noticed that the last two fragments contain a reference to an action to be performed in the near future: "I'll just give him a call", and "I u:h try to get in touch with them." If these conversationalists want to call somebody else, they will have to close the present telephone conversation. Such utterances thus may be seen as one of several moves towards terminating the conversation.

In the following fragment is a reference to a (possible) next call. This utterance is treated as a proposal. D. has phoned the cinema to inquire if he has possibly left his gloves there.

(147) [HvMCD:TC:1:5/2:8]
D. I:'ll have it ch<u>e</u>cked.
(.)
→ D. You can u:h call ag<u>ai</u>n later <u>o</u>n if you like.=
M. =Okay.=
D. =Ja?

→ D. [Fi:ne.
→ M. [Tha:nks.
M. By:e.=
D. =By:e sir.

Not only does D. propose that M. may call again later on, the proposal to call "again later on", implies a proposal to close the present conversation. This double character is also to be found in other proposals for conversation closing; in proposing one thing openly, closing the conversation is proposed by implication. We will now see a rather overt proposal to close the conversation. In fact, speaker only proposes closing the conversation in order to re-open it right away:

(148) [HH:TC:1:22]
→ P. I'll uh uh call you right back, cause the telephone is downstairs >upstairs<, and it's downstairs. We've only got one telephone-set, and that one's next to the bed and the address is downstairs.
H. [Ja.
→ P. [I'll call you right back.=
H. =O:kay.=
P. =Ja?=
H. =Hear you soon then.=
P. =Hear you soon.
P. By:[e.
H. [Thanks.

It will be clear then, that remote proposal sequences are by nature very frequently closing implicative in such a way that they are part of the process of closing down the conversation. The last-positioned "Okay" will be treated both as the closing-object of the remote proposal sequence, and as a proposal for conversation-closing.

4.5.1.1 Foreshortening the closing section

The closing-section of a conversation may be much longer than an "Okay"-exchange plus a terminal greeting-exchange. Between the last-positioned "Okay" and the terminating greeting sequence, some more closing work may be done; especially thankings (see Fr 146, 147), wishes of sorts ("keep smiling", "give my regards to Ann", "have a nice holiday", etc.), and most of all a "see you" or "hear you"-exchange (see Fr 143, 148). Rather than terminating a conversation a "see you" or "hear you"-exchange precedes the terminating "bye"-exchange (see Van Gils 1985 and Driessen & Van Mierlo 1986 on Dutch closing sections) [19].

A closing section may be extended as well as foreshortened. A foreshortening may be realized in such a way that one initiative utterance (a first pair-part) is used both as an initiative and as a response to the prior initiative. Or, from a different perspective, an initiative may be followed by a next initiative, without the response to the first initiative being produced.

This foreshortening may also affect the five-part proposal sequence. For example, the third-positioned "Ja?" may be followed by an utterance which has its natural place later on in the closing section, e.g. a "Thanks" or a "See you". For example:

```
(149) [HvMCD:TC:1:5]
      M. Okay.=
      D. =Ja?
 →    M. Thanks.
```

The sequence may also be foreshortened in a different way. A participant may decide not to wait for his co-participant to produce the relevant next utterance, but may produce two or more subsequent 'own' utterances in a series. This happens in the last fragment, as will become clear when we see the next utterance of that fragment:

```
(150) [HvMCD:TC:1:5]
      M. Okay.=
 →    D. =Ja? [Fi:ne.
      M.      [Thanks.
```

Since M.'s "Thanks" is produced simultaneously with D.'s "Fi:ne", this "Fi:ne" comes right after the "Ja?", I will give further examples where a speaker produces several turns one after the other, without giving his co-participant the time to respond.

```
(151) [HH:TC:15:244]
      V. [Okay:.
 →    M. [Ja?= =Tha:nks.= =By:e.
         ((END OF TAPING)) [20]


(152) [HH:TC:14:339]
      M. I'll come over to yours.
      G. O:kay.=
```

→ M. =Ja? [By:e.
G. [Till then. By:e.

(153) [HH:TC:14:0]
M. You'll be hearing from me again this afternoon.
A. Ja:. Fine.
→ M. Ja:? Good lu:ck.=
A. =Well, by:e.
M. By:e.

These fragments show that once a "Ja?" has been produced, the conversation may be very near its close, especially since the initial speaker who produces this "Ja?", may not await recipient's response, but may rather immediately continue making further closing-moves. Also when it is clear that there is nothing more to say, i.e. there are no further topics to be discussed, this "Ja?" seems to be merely a routine rather than a request-for-confirmation, or an invitation to initiate further details of the proposed action. This means then that once it is clear that the last proposal sequence which has as one of its functions, or even as its main function, to propose closing of the conversation is in progress, the sequence may be worked through very quickly. And the sequence may be worked through so fast, that it is hard to prevent it from turning into a final termination of the conversation.

It has been shown in this section that remote proposal sequences tend to constitute the initiation of the closing section. The sequence-closing "Okay" will then be responded to by a second "Okay", with which the first "Okay" is treated as a proposal for closing. This then makes further closing work relevant. There is a tendency to foreshorten the closing section to such an extent that the five-part sequence is not totally produced. The sequence-positions may be filled with utterances which derive from a later part of the closing section (e.g. a "Thanks" placed in fourth sequence-position as a response to the "Ja?").

It is important for the argument in the next section to stress that these proposal sequences easily turn into the near-termination of the conversation. It is due to this character of the sequence that conversationalists may prefer not to go through the proposal sequence entirely when they do not want to find themselves near the end of the conversation.

4.5.2 Unfinished sequences

In the data we find proposal sequences which start off as five-part sequences. After third or fourth position however, one of the participants may cut off the sequence by introducing a new topic. The reason for this cutting off an ongoing sequence seems to be the closing-relevance of the confirmation of the acceptance. If there is another topic to talk about, one may introduce it before having found oneself about to close the conversation.

I will show some sequences that are cut off after the third-positioned request-for-confirmation [21].

(154) [HH:TC:31:5/238]
C. Would you do that as <u>soon</u> as possible?
(0.9)
C. And let me know when it's ready?
A. Ja: okay.
C. Ja?
→ A. By the way, I've received a ...

The sequence is cut off after speaker's request to confirm the prior acceptance. Instead of responding to this request, recipient (now becoming speaker) initiates a new topic: "By the way, I received a ...", and for some time this new topic will be discussed.

As is the case in the next fragments, this new topic is marked as new and unrelated to the preceding topic, here by means of a 'disjunct marker' (Jefferson 1978a) "by the way" [22]. A disjunct marker signals that the next talk will not be topically coherent with the prior talk. [23]

In the following fragment the new topic, initiated after the request-for-confirmation, is marked as a 'next' topic. It may be noted that the initial sequence is part of speaker's reason-for-calling, i.e. requesting R. to tell the members of tonight's meeting that speaker is unable to be present. When initiating his reason-for-calling the caller has given no indication that there will be any other topic, which defines the conversation as in principle monotopical, so that the first topic is also the last and closing relevant one.

(155) [HH:TC:31:207]
R. I'll pass it on man.=
S. =Ja.=
R. =Ja?
→ S. Furthermore, I've (.) more or less promised...

By starting the new topic by this "furthermore", speaker S. redefines the preceding topic as one in a series, instead of as the only and therefore the last one, as it seemed to be at first. In fact something similar is the case in fragment 154. This sequence is also part of the topic which was caller's reason-for-calling. There, too, the caller had not given any indication that there would be more than just one topic to be discussed. And so when the matter seems to have been dealt with, the conversation seems about to be closed off. But then it turns out that the initial recipient, i.e. the answerer, has a topic as well, which he now introduces before the caller gets the chance to make moves towards further closing of the conversation.

The same happens in the next fragment. Speaker M. has called to V. to tell her that he would like to come round shortly, and before this in principle monotopical conversation can be closed down, answerer V. comes up with a topic herself:

(156) [HH:TC:15:11]
M. I'll come on your bicycle then,
(0.9)
V. Ja::.=
M. =and I'll bring the car back with me.
(0.3)
V. O:h, that fine as well.
M. Ja:?
(1.5)
→ V. We:: u::hm saw Ysbrand's here now, and ...

Again recipient cuts off the ongoing closing implicative sequence to initiate a new and unrelated topic. This topic is not marked as unrelated by a disjunct marker, as was done in the previous instances. V. uses a different device; instead of responding to the request-for-confirmation she waits for 1.5 seconds and then starts talking about something else. As Maynard (1980) has shown long pauses often precede topic changes and they constitute environments for new topic beginnings. Conversationalist V. may be seen as creating such an environment in this way, making it possible to introduce a new topic smoothly.

These fragments all start off with some sort of proposal, which is responded to with an acceptance. Then the first speaker requests confirmation of this acceptance, usually with a "Ja?". And instead of providing the relevant response, which would have made the sequence - and conversation - ready for closing, recipient initiates a new topic. On one occasion this is done by first creating a long pause, on other occasions by marking the new topic as being unrelated to the prior one: "by the way", "furthermore", or by some other formulation.

In initiating a new topic rather than providing the solicited response to the "Ja?", recipient prevents the sequence shading off into the closing of the conversation. As has been pointed out earlier, these five-part sequences are closing implicative, and they are especially so when no indication has been given that the present topic will not be the last one. On several occasions Sacks points out, if a speaker wants to indicate that the next utterance-completion should not be treated as the completion of the turn and a turn transitional place, the speaker should indicate so before coming to this first next utterance-completion (e.g. Sacks 1971, Chapter 3 on 'utterance incompletors' and Chapter 4 on 'multi-clause signals'; cf. also 3.2 on 'larger projects').

A similar procedure seems to be at issue here with respect to completion of the topical section of the conversation: if there is any other topic to be discussed one should signal that before the topical section has shaded off into the closing section. And since the transition between these two sections of the conversation may be realized smoothly in the course of the second part of the five-part sequence, speakers have to cut off the sequence in time.

This analysis sheds a new light on the conversational function of the third-positioned "Ja?". It was shown earlier that a "Ja?" is not only a request-for-confirmation of the prior acceptance, but also invites the recipient to discuss further possible details and particulars of the action to be performed. When the recipient does not have any further questions or remarks, he may confirm the acceptance, after which the sequence may be closed off by the speaker.

The unfinished sequences as we have seen them in this subsection however, suggest that a "Ja?" may also be responded to with a new and unrelated topic. This is reminiscent of Schegloff & Sacks, who say that by the term possible pre-closing, they indicate that this strategy is used "not only possibly to initiate a closing section, but also, by inviting the insertion of unmentioned mentionables, to provide for the reopening of topic talk." (1973:247). The question then becomes whether we might see this "Ja?" not only as a possible pre-closing of the present sequence as such (i.e. if responded to by a confirmation, the sequence will be terminated), but also as a possible pre-closing of, or as the first move towards, the closing of the entire conversation. In the discussion on the foreshortening of this sequence it already became clear that this "Ja?" may be responded to by the recipient producing an utterance which has its 'natural' place further down in the closing section, like a "Thanks" or a "Bye bye". This is especially the case when the current topic is in principle the last and a closing implicative topic.

What we may say then, is that although such a "Ja?" perhaps is not a possible conversation pre-closing object in the first place, it may under certain conditions be treated as such.

Thus a third-positioned "Ja?" may have several hierarchically ordered interactional functions. It 1) provides room for further questions and remarks about the proposed action, or if there is no more to add to the proposed action, it is 2) a request-for-confirmation of the prior acceptance. If the topic is a last topic, it 3) provides for the initiation of as yet unmentioned mentionables. And if there is nothing else to talk about, either with respect to either the present topic or some other topic, it may be treated as 4) a possible conversation pre-closing object.

5 Summary and Conclusion

The work presented here results from the analysis of the sequential structure and the interactional function of remote proposal-acceptance sequences as they occur in mundane Dutch telephone conversations. The research question addressed in this book is how conversationalists proceed sequentially and interactionally in order to etablish a deal with respect to a proposal to perform some sort of action in the future.

The subject of the research is constituted by a range of initiative-response action sequences such as proposals, requests, invitations, suggestions, promises, offers, and their acceptances. These initiative actions are classed under the general label 'proposals for remote action', or 'remote proposals'. Remote proposals purport to request the addressee to perform, or collaborate with, some action in the future, e.g. attending a party, delivering a message somewhere, etc. Remote proposals are distinguished from immediate proposals, which concern actions to be performed immediately. In telephone conversations, this usually means calling someone else to the telephone.

The recipient of a proposal is requested to accept and comply with the proposed action. However whereas immediate proposals can and should be complied with right after the time of delivery, remote proposals can for the time being, just be accepted by the recipient, i.e. the recipient can just say or give an indication that he will comply with it. The factual performance can take place later on. This difference seems to be a possible explanation of the structural difference between the two types of proposal sequences. Whereas immediate proposal sequences have a three-part structure, remote proposal sequences turn out to have a five-part structure.

Sequential implicativeness

Generally speaking, research in Conversation Analysis

(CA) is interested in the procedures by which conversationalists produce their own behaviour, and understand and deal with the behaviour of others. It is strongly focussed on the sequential organisation of conversation. Utterances, i.e. actions, do not stand on their own, but require and project a relevant next action by the co-participant. This phenomenon is referred to as the sequential implicativeness of a turn's talk (Schegloff & Sacks 1973).

In its strongest form, this projection of a next action may be accomplished through adjacency pairs. An adjacency pair is a sequence of two utterances, which are

1. adjacently ordered,
2. produced by different speakers,
3. divided into a first pair-part and a second pair-part,
4. typed, so that a first pair-part makes the occurrence of the second pair-part expectable.

Adjacency pairs are exemplified by question-answer sequences, request-acceptance/rejection sequences, "Hello" and "Goodbye" sequences, etc. For example, the question-answer sequence:

(157) [HH:TC:1:2]
      1 H. Were you already in bed?
      2 K. Oh no.

In this book however, proposal-acceptance sequences are not seen as adjacency pairs in the sense above. An immediate proposal-acceptance sequence is claimed to be a three-part sequence, and a remote proposal-acceptance sequence to be a five-part sequence. For example, the fragment given above as an example of an adjacency pair, i.e. of a two-part question-answer sequence, has a third-positioned acknowledgement:

(158) [HH:TC:1:2]
      1 K. Were you already in bed?
      2 H. Oh no.
→   3 K. O(h)o(h)o.

This third-positioned utterance not only acknowledges the answer to the question, it also closes off the sequence. The adjacency triplet has the following sequential structure:

1 speaker : initiation
2 recipient: response
3 speaker : acknowledgement/sequence closing

This structure holds at least for question-answer sequences, repair sequences, and immediate proposal sequences. In the next example the initial utterance is a request to call someone else to the telephone:

(159) [HH:TC:5:13]
1 Caller : Is Annet around?=
2 Answerer: =Ja sure.=
3 Caller : =Okay.

This request is accepted by the recipient, upon which the requester acknowledges the acceptance. This acknowledgement closes off the sequence, and thus makes room for a next activity, in this case the compliance with the request, i.e. calling Annet.

Utterances like "Is So-and-So there?", when produced very early in telephone conversations, are requests to call So-and-So to the telephone, although they are formulated as inquiries. Such inquiries function as prerequests, i.e. by producing them speakers determine whether it makes sense to initiate the intended request to ask for So-and-So. However when So-and-So is indeed there, recipients treat such an inquiry as the as yet unstated request.

Rather than, or apart from saying something like "Ja sure", recipients may indicate that they are in the process of calling So-and-So, for example:

(160) [PtH:TC:24]
1 Caller : Is Henk Brandon around?
(.)
→ 2 Answerer: One moment please.

The recipient may also respond to such an initial utterance in two ways; he may first treat the utterance as an inquiry by indicating that the person asked for is indeed in, and he may immediately proceed to treat the very same utterance as a request. This in fact happens in the prior conversation:

(161) [PtH:TC:24]
Caller : Is Henk Brandon around?
(.)
→ Answerer: Ja, he's here.
→ Answerer: One moment please.

Two rules of interpretation and production have been formulated with respect to initial utterances such as the ones in fragment 160 and 161:

1. If, in the opening of a telephone conversation, the caller inquires whether some named person is in, this inquiry is heard as a request to call that person to the telephone.
2. When such an inquiry is answered with affirmative, and without further modification, this is heard as the acceptance of the unstated request to call that person to the telephone.

Apart from three-part immediate proposal sequences we find remote proposal sequences, which have a five-part structure, such as:

```
(162) [HH:TC:12:9]
      1 F. But come over here, so we can
           all talk about It in peace.=
      2 M. =Fine.
              (0.5)
      3 F. Ja?=
      4 M. =I'll be there in a minute.=
      5 F. =O:kay.
```

The remote proposal sets up a five-part sequence, constructed of two adjacently positioned initiation-response sequences, and an acknowledgement token, which closes off the entire sequence.

The sequence starts off with the proposal to come over to the speaker's home. When the recipient accepts this proposal, the initial speaker makes a request-for-confirmation. In response to this, the recipient confirms his earlier acceptance ("Fine.") by indicating "I'll be there in a minute.". This confirmation is acknowledged by the initial speaker, by which he also closes off the sequence. Thus the remote proposal sequence is:

```
1 speaker  :  proposal
2 recipient:  acceptance
3 speaker  :  request-for-confirmation
4 recipient:  confirmation
5 speaker  :  acknowledgement/sequence closing
```

This five-part sequence is similar to the three-part immediate proposal/acceptance sequence, except that an extra sequence, i.e. the request-for-confirmation/ confirmation, is built in.

Accepting proposals

So far I have talked about proposals which are accepted by recipients. However proposals have alternative responses, i.e. they may be accepted or rejected. And as the literature on the so-called preference organization shows, accepting a proposal is preferred to rejecting it. The ways in which rejections and acceptances are formulated differ. Acceptances tend to be produced right after the proposal, whereas rejections are often prefaced by a stated acceptance ("Ja, but..."), or they are produced with all sorts of delays: filled or unfilled pauses, or they may be preceded by utterances by which the recipient withholds acceptance or rejection, such as a request-for-clarification or a request-for-repetition ("What?", "Hm?") (cf. Pomerantz 1984a, Davidson 1984).

Delay devices are said to be rejection implicative, i.e. in principle they project rejection. However they may be followed by an acceptance nevertheless. This seems to be mainly due to the fact that the proposer, after having noticed his recipient's hesitation to accept the proposal, tends to produce an alternative and perhaps a stronger version of the initial proposal, which will be accepted.

This procedure has as its consequence that a proposal is not an action which is produced by the initial speaker only, but that it is an 'interactionally achieved proposal'. This also holds for proposals which are accepted right away, since in such cases the recipients may be seen as having made no use of the opportunity to influence the proposal.

Since the withholding of the acceptance tends not to be followed by a final rejection of the proposal, because the initial speaker may come up with an alternative or a stronger proposal, I have treated these withholdings as 'non-acceptances', or 'not-yet-acceptances'. Rather than indicating that they are in the process of rejecting the proposal, recipients may be seen as displaying that they may accept the proposal if it is made more suitable for acceptance.

Once the proposal has been accepted, the initial speaker will solicit confirmation of this acceptance, mostly by a "Ja?", and the recipient will confirm his acceptance. Then the sequence will be closed off by the proposer.

Response forms

It has become clear however, that the request-for-confirmation only follows after certain formulations of the response, e.g. "No problem", "Ja sure", "Ja of course", "that's alright", etc. Such responses have been called full acceptance-forms (cf. Pomerantz 1984a).

As it turned out, there are other forms of responses which are not followed by a request-for-confirmation, i.e. they are treated by the speaker as 'weak acceptances' or 'non-acceptances'.

When the recipient produces a single "Ja", the speaker will extend the initial utterance, and thus solicit a new response. A "Ja" in response to a proposal is thus treated by the speaker as a weak acceptance or a non-acceptance. Not only speakers treat a "Ja" as a non-acceptance form, recipients also show a normative orientation to a single "Ja" not being enough for the acceptance of a proposal. Recipients may start producing a "Ja.", wait for a while, and when speaker does not extend his initial proposal, they may add "very well", "Of course", and the like. For example:

(163) [HH:TC:12:12]
M. Then I'll send him on to you straight away.
(.)
→ F. Ja.
(0.4)
→ F. Very well.
M. Ja?

Since "Ja" is a conversationally ambiguous word, it is very apt for doing negotiation work. It may initially be used as a continuer, indicating that the speaker is recognized as having, or supposed not to have, completed his proposal yet. But when the speaker does not continue talking about the proposal in the pause following the "Ja", this "Ja" may retrospectively be 'redefined' as a full acceptance, in that the recipient adds a "Very well", or some other acceptance-completing item. Not only a "Ja"-receipt may solicit further talking about the initial proposal, this also holds for silences, "Oh"-receipts, and (partial) repeats of the prior utterance.

Dealing with weak acceptance-forms

When the proposal is not fully accepted, the initial speaker deals with this in at least three ways:

(1) Weak acceptance-forms are often treated by proposers as the recipient having some trouble accepting the

proposal. The speaker's candidate analysis of the possible trouble may be shown in the subsequent proposal-turn. The absence of the acceptance may, for example, be treated by the speaker as if recipient has not understood the gist of the proposal:

```
(164) [HH:TC2:85]
      proposal S. Then it would be very convenient for
                  us if you came up to the 7th of July.
      repeat   R. July.=
               S. =Ja.
→     clarify  S. So to have you until.
```

Or the recipient may be supposed to be unable to accept the proposal which, in the next instance, concerns the suggested time of the meeting:

```
(165) [HH:TC 14:399]
      proposal S. Is that possible? Thursday afternoon.
      silence        (1.1)
→     trouble  S. Or would I be too late then?
```

It has been pointed out by several authors that the accounts which recipients give for refusing proposals, especially requests or invitations, tend to cluster around the issue of ability rather than around the recipient's willingness to comply with the proposal (Merritt 1976, Labov & Fanshel 1977, Levinson 1983, Drew 1984). It is also striking that the initial speaker may question the recipient's ability to comply as a possible explanation for the recipient's withholding acceptance of the proposal.

The reference to the recipient's (in)ability to comply with the proposal is parallelled by one of the preconditions Labov & Fanshel (1977) have formulated for the rule of making a valid request:

> "If A addresses to B an imperative specifying an action X at the time T1, and B believes that A believes that
> 1a. X should be done (for a purpose Y)
> 1b. B would not do X in the absence of the request
> → 2. B has the ability to do X
> 3. B has the obligation to do X or is willing to do it.
> 4. A has the right to tell B to do X.
> then A is heard as making a valid request for action." (Op. cit:78)

(2) The initial speaker, not having received a (full)

acceptance, often goes on to account for the reason the proposal is made or, why it is made this way:

```
(166) [HH:TC:20:10]
      proposal   A. I wanted to ask if u:hm you could
                    ((drop the key)) at A:ns's, (.)
                    in Heartstreet.
      silence         (1.3)
      weak acc.  R. O:h.
                    (...)
→     account    A. .hh 'Cause Ans, she's coming to uh
                    stay here when we're on holiday.
                      (.)
      acc.       R. O::h ja:. Well fi:ne.
```

This account concerns the "purpose" as formulated in Labov & Fanshel's precondition: "X should be done (for a purpose Y)".

It has become clear that, if recipients do not fully accept the proposal, it is most likely for speakers to account for the proposal. Recipients tend to respond to this in two ways. As in the last fragment, they may first produce an "O::h ja:"-like response, by which they indicate that the initial proposal was unclear, and they may then accept the proposal by e.g., "Well fi:ne".

The fact that proposers tend to account for their as-yet-unaccepted proposals, and that recipients respond to the account in the way described above, has led to the conclusion that proposals are to be accounted for when the account is not apparent. Proposals are seen as composed of [account] + [proposal]. The account is either apparent, or explicitly provided by the proposer.

Proposals are usually accounted for in the preface of the proposal, in which speakers may, e.g. state a problem, after which they will come up with proposal, which may solve this problem. The next fragment of a conversation between friends is an example of this. The account/pre-request has been arrowed and the request has been double-arrowed.

```
(167) [HH:TC: 18:46]
      L. Hey I've got another questio:n,
      R. Ja:.
→     L. U:h I've got a little problem, I've got
         to do some washing,
      R. Ja:.
→     L. and actually I can't leave the house,
         because (.) I'm on sick-leave, (.) and I
         think it's risky to be out in the streets.
```

R. Ja:.
→→ L. So I'd like to ask you if I could do my
washing at your place.

The request is being led up to in an elegant way. The speaker starts with the announcement "Hey I got another questio:n.". The next step is mentioning "a little problem", which is then clarified. This explanation of the problem is the preface to and the account of the final request: "So I'd like to ask you if I could do my washing at your place.".

(3) The third way in which speakers deal with the withholding of a full acceptance is just 'prompting' a new response, for example:

(168) [PtH:TC:3.5.79]

	proposal	G.	But don't mind these girls and stick to your friend and uh (.) call them names.
	weak acc.	C.	Jha.
→	prompt	G.	Right?

On the willingness and the ability to accept

What has been discussed so far is mainly the first part of the sequence, i.e. the proposal and its acceptance. In fact the acceptance is an in-principle-acceptance. In this stage of the interaction, co-participants are dealing with the recipient's willingness to go along with the proposed action. We often find a "would you" in the proposing-utterance:

(169) [HH:TC:33:33]
1 K. But would you do that?
(0.6)
2 Z. Ja:. (.) Of course.

A recipient may be willing to perform the action, and may thus accept the proposal, but he may find out only later when he has heard more details, that he is unable to comply with it after all.

The second part of the sequence is devoted to this aspect of the proposal, i.e. to the ability to perform the proposed action. When the proposal has in principle been accepted, the speaker will say "Ja?". This utterance is a request to confirm the initial acceptance, but at the same time it provides room for discussing details and particularities of the action proposed. For example:

(170) [HH:TC:30:33]
      1 K. But would you do that?
           (0.6)
      2 Z. Ja:. (.) Of course.
      3 K. Ja?
           (1.1)
→   Z. Can it be done with u:h (machine).
           Or wha:t?

A recipient may not wait for the request-for-confirmation, and may initiate such further questions right after his initial acceptance:

(171) [HH:TC:20:7]
      1 R. Maybe you would ask her to call me:?
           (0.3)
      2 H. Ja:. I can do that.=
→   H. =What's your number?

When this inserted talk is finished, the recipient will produce a new acceptance-utterance, which will be reacted to again by speaker's "Ja?". In recycling part of the sequence in this way, the co-participants provide a next opportunity to initiate a next question or remark with respect to the action to be performed. This procedure makes it possible to discuss all the aspects of the proposed action before the sequence is closed off, and a new topic is introduced.

This becomes especially clear in, for example, telephone calls to a doctor or dentist in which an appointment is made. When the initial request for the appointment has been accepted, further details of the appointment will follow before the sequence has been closed off. These details tend to be initiated in the form of subsidiary proposal sequences. We may thus find a structure such as:

1 Proposal (e.g. Could I please come?)
2 Acceptance
3 Request-for-confirmation
1 Proposal (e.g. Today?)
2 Acceptance
3 Request-for-confirmation
1 Proposal (e.g. Twelve o'clock?)
.
.
.
5 Acknowledgement and sequence closing

The five-part structure of the remote proposal sequence thus plays an important part in the establishment of the topical coherence of the conversation, and makes for a smooth conversational organisation.

Demonstrating acceptance

Another important aspect of the second part of the sequence is the formulation of the response to the request-for-confirmation. Whereas the initial acceptance tends to be formulated as "Ja sure", "Sure, no problem" etc., the confirmation, i.e. the re-acceptance utterance, tends to be formulated differently. Whereas in second sequence position recipients claim acceptance, in fourth position they use formulations by which they display their 'sincerity' in accepting the proposal. Recipients may use formulations which suggest that they are already in the process of executing the action, for example:

(172) [HH:TC:12:9]
      1 F. But come over here, so we can
           all talk about It in peace.=
      2 M. =Fine.
            (0.5)
      3 F. Ja?=
→   4 M. =I'll be there in a minute.=
      5 F. =Okay.

Or they may provide other pieces of evidence that they will indeed comply: saying that they are making a note right now, checking the address they are asked to visit or the telephone number they are asked to dial, etc.

The proposers may signal later on that they treat the acceptance as a convincing acceptance, and that they consider themselves to have established a deal with respect to the action which has been proposed. This becomes clear in the following fragment, of which the sequence-closing acknowledgement is followed by "See you then.":

(173) [HH:TC:12:9]
      F. But come over here, so we can
         all talk about In peace.=
      M. =Fine.
          (0.5)
      F. Ja?=
      M. =I'll be there in a minute.=

F. =Okay.
→ F. See you then.

Or, after the recipient has accepted the speaker's invitation to attend his party on Sunday around three o'clock, the co-participants will come to treat that discussion as now having established an arrangement. After the sequence, and just before they come to the closing of the conversation, we find:

(174) [HH:TC:5:483]
H. Hey listen. I'm going to call
some other people.
A. Ja:.
→ H. Then I'll see you on Sunday.
A. Ja.
H. Ja?
A. Ja: [okay.
H. [Around three o'clock.
→ A. Ja, I've written it down.
H. O::kay.

In some fragments the recipient gives even stronger evidence that he has sincerely accepted the proposal. After having confirmed his initial acceptance in the fourth sequence-position, a recipient may later on treat this utterance as a promise or an offer to execute the very same action. In the next fragment the initial sequence proceeds regularly, but when the speaker acknowledges the confirmation with an "O:kay:", the recipient treats this "O:kay:" as if it were the acceptance of his prior utterance:

(175) [HH:TC:27:3]
1 F. U:h would it be possible for you to come
tomorrow (...) at two, half past two?
(4.5)
2 M. Ja: su:re.
((embedded talk))
4 M. I'll be at yours at two o'clock.
(0.6)
→ 5 F. O:kay:.=
3 M. =Ja:?=
4 F. =Ja, we'll do: tha:t.=
M. =See you tomorro:w.

The recipient's re-acceptance and the speaker's acknowledgement retrospectively function as an offer or promise and its acceptance, which together constitute the following structure:

1 proposal		
2 acceptance		
3 request-for-confirmation		
4 confirmation	=	1 offer/promise
5 acknowledgement	=	2 acceptance
		3 request-for-confirmation
		4 confirmation
		5 acknowledgement

Turning one's acceptance of a proposal to do something into an offer to perform that very same action, and thus turning one's passive role of recipient of a proposal into the active role of an offerer, may be looked upon as strong evidence that the initial recipient will comply with the proposal.

It is clear that some of the rules or preconditions for making proposals, here mostly requests, as they have been formulated by, among others, Searle (1969), and Labov & Fanshel (1977), come to the surface of the interaction. Not only do speakers who make a proposal believe that recipients are willing and able to carry out the proposed action, this is what is being dealt with in the sequence. Co-participants will first deal with the proposal and their willingness to accept it. Once this has been done, they may discuss further details of the proposed action, and the ability to perform it, and finally accept the proposal.

Furthermore, if the recipient's willingness to comply is not just a speaker's assumption, recipients themselves tend to display that they are indeed willing to do what they have been asked to do.

Labov & Fanshel's statement that "the action should be done (for a purpose of Y)", becomes manifest in the interaction when the speaker accounts for the proposal, either voluntary in the pre-sequence, or after having found the recipient not accepting the proposal.

On the basis of the analysis provided in this book, two changes in Labov & Fanshel's rule of request may be suggested. First, the parentheses in "X should be done (for a purpose Y)" may be left out, since conversationalists turn out to be normatively oriented to speaker providing an account. Secondly, whereas Labov & Fanshel (as well as Searle) first mention the recipient's ability, and then his willingness, these two aspects may be turned around.

Unfinished sequences

Although the remote proposal sequence has been described as a five-part sequence, examples can be found where the proposal does not set up five, or even four successive turns. These instances have been analyzed as unfinished five-part sequences.

Part of the analysis concerns the fact that these sequences often occur as topics which are typically 'last topics', initiating the closing of the conversation. It turns out that the closing section may be foreshortened in such a way that the five-part sequence becomes part of the closing. Especially the "Ja?" may be followed by utterances which have their 'natural' place in the closing section. In some cases we found a "Bye bye" in response to a "Ja?". The next fragment shows how quickly the conversation may proceed:

```
(176) [HH:TC:14:339]
      1 M. I'll come over to your's.
      2 G. Ō:kay.=
      3 M. =Ja?
→       M. [By:e
        G. [See you soon then. By:e.
```

It has been argued therefore, that a possible reason for conversationalists cutting off the sequence before its completion, is that they want to prevent finding themselves near the closing of the conversation. When one of the co-participants has some other topic to be discussed, he may initiate it right after this third-positioned "Ja?".

For that reason it was suggested that under certain circumstances, especially if the topic is a last topic, this "Ja?" not only solicits a confirmation of the acceptance or further talk about details of the proposed action, it may also be heard as a proposal to close the conversation. This "Ja?" may thus be seen as a possible pre-closing object in the way Schegloff & Sacks (1973) use the notion, i.e. as an object which provides further conversational closing work, as well as for the introduction of as yet 'unmentioned mentionables' such as, for example, details of the action being proposed, or a new and unrelated topic.

After a detailed analysis of the remote proposal sequences, it became clear why they are five-part sequences, rather than only two- or three-part sequences. Since the proposal concerns an action to be performed later on, recipients are not in a position to be able to show their compliance right away, as they are in the case of immediate proposals. And rather than complying with the proposal, recipients first accept the proposal (e.g. "Ja fine"), and then demonstrate that they will indeed comply (e.g. "I'll be there in a minnit").

The second ground for looking upon the remote proposal as a five-part sequence is that in that way it makes possible a discussion of details of the action to be performed; mostly how, when, and where the action is to be carried out. It may happen that, although the recipient has said that he is willing to perform the action, he may turn out to be unable to do it, once he hears the details. This may then lead to a final rejection of the proposal, or to further negotiations about the initial proposal. For example, the proposal to go to the cinema may still be accepted although it will not be on Monday, as was initially proposed and accepted, but on Wednesday.

In terms of speech act theory, this study may be considered an analysis of the 'illocutionary act complex' (van Eemeren & Grootendorst 1982), i.e. the 'cooperative illocutionary act' (Hancher 1979), of proposal-acceptance. This cooperative illocutionary act, i.e. action sequence has been analyzed and described in terms of how it is interactionally achieved by the conversationalists rather than as a conversational form as such.

I would like to close with a quotation of Schegloff (1982:89): "If certain stable forms appear to emerge or recur in talk, they should be understood as an orderliness wrested by the participants from interactional contingency, rather than as automatic products of standardized plans. Form, one might say, is also the distillate of action and/in interaction, not only its blueprint. If that is so, then the description of forms of behavior, forms of discourse (such as stories) included, has to include interaction among their constitutive domains, and not just as the stage on which scripts written in the mind are played out.".

Footnotes

NOTES TO CHAPTER 1

1. In many cases in the text that follows, the personal pronouns 'he' and 'she' refer to specific speakers. However when the generic pronoun 'he' is mentioned, where that does not apply to a specific speaker, I mean this to read as 'he' and 'she', i.e. none of the findings reported in this book show any systematic differences according to the gender of speakers.

NOTES TO CHAPTER 2

1. Compare Bergmann's attack on the German treatment of CA (Bergmann 1981).

2. Sacks (S' 1966, 1972a) claims that members of a culture make use of various categories when they select identifications for other members. By "categorization device" is meant; a "collection of membership categories" [e.g. 'family'], "containing at least a category, that may be applied to some population," [mother, father, child] "containing at least a Member, so as to provide, by the use of some rules of application, for the pairing of at least a population Member and a categorization device member. A 'device' is then an 'collection' plus rules of application." (1972a:32).

   A person may belong to several categories, i.e. sex, occupation, age group, family, etc. Sacks says that: "It would not be a question of simply finding that Device which fits persons at hand, but, more importantly, the problem is 'which of several appropriate devices is to be used'." (1966:17). The task is that now the "relevantly correct" device should be found and formulated, i.e. is a certain person 'Maggy's father', 'husband', 'manager', 'negro', etc.

   An important characteristic of membership categories is that they are a conventional basis for attributing so-called "category-bound activities" to persons. With respect to Wilson's example, this means that when somebody identifies with "midcity emergensee:", he defines himself as a person who is to be addressed for the type of problems emergency centres solve.

NOTES TO CHAPTER 3

1. In linguistics an utterance is defined as the unique product of its syntactic structure (Dik & Kooij 1979: 29). In CA however, the notion of utterance is used rather loosely; it sometimes seems to refer to a 'turn', on other occasions it is used in a linguistic sense, for example, in a word as 'multi-utterance turn'.

2. See also Goffman (1976) on the 'working agreement', which is an agreement "for all practical purposes". Goffman says that "A respondent cannot make evident that he has understood 'the' meaning of a statement, because in a sense there isn't one. All he can do is respond to what he can display as 'a' meaning that will carry - although, of course, he may effectively sustain the impression (and himself believe) that his 'a' is 'the'." (Goffman 1976:45).

3. When talking about such larger turns, Sacks says that "You signal that the forthcoming utterance is not to be constrained by its sentence-structure - its being a sentence, or two sentences, etc.- but is to be attended by reference to their alternative units that have completions, and have routinely recognizable completions." (Sacks, Oct.26.1967, L4, part 2:4-5).

4. Some restrictions on turn-taking are formulated in case of production of a Discourse Unit. A DU is produced by the 'primary speaker' (PS), and the co-participant is named the 'DU recipient' (DR). The restrictions on the turn-taking model are the following:
   R(a) The PS is expected to continue a DU until a turn-constructional unit which marks DU completion has been produced.
   R(b1) The DU is sequentially implicative for the kind of contributions DR's can make ("DU-accompanying actions"). These actions are preferably of limited length.
   R(b2) DR-contributions should be placed according to the turn-taking model, i.e., around the end of turn-constructional units.

R(c) If there is speaker-transition at a point which is marked as DU-incomplete, there is a preference for the PS to become next speaker. Thus, during a DU-in-progress, nobody else starts another DU. (Houtkoop & Mazeland 1985:601).

5. This is an educational imperative, and not a conversational one, as Goffman (1976:54) states.

6. An utterance is sequentially ambiguous because it is 'empirically ambiguous' (Schegloff 1984:36), that is, an utterance may be heard as, for example, a question or a request, and it may thus receive either an answer or an acceptance/rejection as its relevant next action.

7. Maynard (1980) circumscribes a topic change as talk which is "unrelated to talk in prior turns in that they utilize new referents, and thus implicate and occasion a series of utterances constituting a different line of talk." (1980:264), whereas a topic shift is "a move from one aspect of a topic to another to occasion a different set of mentionables." (1980: 271).

8. Severinson Eklundh & Linell (1983) discuss three-part structures in face-to-face conversation. They give as an (artificial) example:

   1 B. Hello, Jim.
   2 A. Hello
   3 A & B. ((joint confirming eye-contact))

9. The fact that identification and greeting sequences are considered as consisting of a first and a second pair-part, may be due to the fact that they have been analyzed in telephone conversation data rather than in face-to-face materials. The assumed ordering of the two actions therefore is an artefact of the 'distribution rules' (who speaks when and does what. cf. Schegloff, 1968), in telephone conversation rather than an intrinsic feature of these paired actions.

10 A reciprocal pair should not be confused with what Edmondson calls a 'reciprocal exchange', the latter being "an exchange whose outcome may be said to 'reciprocate' the outcome of a preceding exchange, which it therefore reciprocates." (Edmondson 1981: 111). For example,

[Edmondson 1981:112, simplified]
1 X. what's your name
2 Y. Margaret
1
2 X. uh well mine's David

It will be clear, however, that there is a strong conceptual relationship between the two notions.

11 Lynch (1979) speaks of "achieved agreement" (versus "implicit agreement" as this notion is used in social science).

12 Compare Sacks on 'slave-master talk' in America's Pre-Civil War South, where "agreeing with any utterance that could be made was a required thing such that that set up games of trying to get a slave to be found to disagree. (...) There were some negative consequences as well for the masters in that they could never find out what they wanted to know." (Sacks W' 1970, L4:21-22).

NOTES TO CHAPTER 4

1. When saying "in the opening section of a telephone conversation", I mean in fact 'before caller (perhaps implicitly) gives a reason-for-calling'. In some of the data the utterance "Is So-and-So there?" is produced only rather late in the conversation, but it is nevertheless treated by the answerer as a request to speak to So-and-So. This utterance may be preceded by extensive conversation, but as long as the caller has not given a reason-for-calling, it will be treated as what caller requires from answerer. We may see this signalled in the following fragment. Caller Ricky phones a couple, and the wife answers the telephone. The answerer happens to explain why she herself intended to telephone Ricky. Now this sets up several other topics. After eleven pages of transcript the conversation proceeds as follows: (note that the Dutch "alleen" as it is used in this fragment, means "alone", "by oneself" as well as "lonely").

[HH:TC:20:11]
R. Hey, and is u:h Ronnie home?=
A. =No:.
R. O:ho:h.
A. Hu(h).
R. Hu(h). Are you all alone?= ((in Dutch 'alleen'))

A. =No: ye:s I mean.
R. No ye(h)s.
A. Ha(h)ah. He's in the gara:ge. So I don't feel lonely.= ((in Dutch 'alleen'))
R. =O:h.=
A. =Because he's around the corner.
(0.7)
R. O:h ja.
(0.7)
→ A. Why are you calling then?

If Ricky does not mention any reason-for-calling, and if he treats his inquiry whether Ronny is home as just an inquiry, why has he called "then"? But it turns out that Ricky indeed called to tell something important to Ronny, which he now tells the woman who may pass it on.

The same orientation to a "Is So-and-So home?", as being a request to speak to So-and-So, is to be found in the next extract of a conversation between answerer Peter and his mother-in-law. After a lengthy period of social talk the conversation continues like this:

[HH:TC:22:10)
M. U:h Irene won't be there, will she?
P. Ja, she is there.=
M. =O:h [ja:.
P. [She is there.=
M. =No fine.
→ P. Should I get her for you?
M. Ja: if uh (.) if possible, ja.=
P. =Okay.

Again whereas the caller acts as if she just inquired about Irene being home by acknowledging the positive answer by "O:h ja:.", and "No fine.", Peter nevertheless supposes that she might like to speak to Irene. And indeed, this turns out to be the case.

The interactional function of this type of inquiry strongly depends on the place where it occurs, i.e. its function derives partly from the overall organisation of the conversation.

2. The phrase "positively, and without further qualification" is added in rule 2, since the intended called may be present, though unable to come to the telephone, for example in:

[HH:TC:18:77]
L. Is u:h Mariette still awake?
→ M. Ja: she's in the tub.
(0.8)
L. O(h)och.

[HH:TC:30]
C. Is doctor Marijnsen there?
→ A. He's in a meeting.
C. Oh.

3. It may be clear that I disagree with West who does not include requests for confirmation of a previous item (as well as requests for repair and markers of surprise) "in the general category of questions that call for answers. (...) such objects look rather back than forward in sequential time, and hence they seem dependent for their sense on some equivalent of a first pair part." (West 1983:85).

4. Unlike Ehlich (1979), who used technical equipment for making a phonological analysis in order to study the function of the German "Hm", it is my point of view that the analyst's ear should be enough here, since the conversationalists have only ears for detecting phonological differences.

5. In the fragment below, in which conversationalists talk about a stutter-therapy, is a series of different forms of continuers.

[HH:TC:21:1]
A. But you always pick something up, don't you.
(0.5)
R. Ja: I'm taking the course uh myself now, too,=
→ A. =Ja.
R. uh (0.8) since uh September now,
→ A. Ja:.
R. it's almost over and=
→ A. =Ja ja.
R. and the last meeting will be in about a month then u::h I have to u:h speak=
→ A. =Ja:.
R. no u:h learn to speak fluently.

6. The very last part of this conversation has some peculiarities:

R. Do tell her that please.
D. Ja.

R. Ja?
B. Bye:.
R. Okay::.
R. Bye: Duncan.

When we look into this last part of the conversation, one may think children of this age have not yet mastered this type of sequence, and which types of formulations there are to be used to satisfactorily accept a request. This extract also shows that an adult, or at least this speaker, takes all sequential steps as if her recipient dis so too. Although D. did not produce a fourth-positioned confirmation in response to R.'s "Ja?", but instead a termination-utterance ("Bye:"), nevertheless R. produces a fifth-positioned "Okay". And only then does she come up with a return "Bye: Duncan".

7. In this fragment R's question in line 3 "how will you be going, will you be going by car?", is treated by his co-participant as a pre-selfinvitation. Those lines containing indications for such hearing of the question have been arrowed. Note that speaker himself displays that the question was meant as pre-selfinvitation.

[HH:TC:21:7]
E. You know that you've got to uh play
football tomorrow?
((some lines omitted))
R. U:h in u:h Sloten right?
E. Sloterdijk, right.
(0.7)
E. Do you know [where that is?
R. [How will you be going, will
you be going by car?
E. Ja, I'll be going very early, I do have a
→ car, but I'm leaving at ten already. Because
I have to see some people before.=
R. =Oh ja.
→ In that case I'll go in a different way.
((some lines omitted))
→ E. But if you take the bus, you can drive
u:h back with me.
→ R. Oh ja, that fine. Ja. Please.

8. With the notion 'post-completor' Sacks refers to a "group of objects used in conversation which have as their specific work (a) proposing that the talk that has preceded their use was both a complete utterance

and specifically implicative, and (b) that on their completion, that prior utterance, not having been responded to in spite of the occurrence of a completion that should have been recognized and should have occasioned change, should now be responded to, and (c) that such a response specifically being a response to the prior intendedly recognizable complete and sequentially adequate utterance should also acknowledge the use of the post completor." (Sacks 1971, Chapter 4, 10-11).

Jefferson, furthermore, talks of a 'post response completion response solicitation'. "The response solicitation may work as a prompting of some more elaborate response, not merely re-relinquishing the floor, but indicate to recipient the sort of talk he ought to be doing with the turn he had relinquished and is now being re-proferred." (Jefferson 1981a:20-21).

9. Merritt (1976) refers to such "What?" as a "call for replay", or a "rerun signal". Sacks & Schegloff (1979) talk about a "repair initiator".

10 See also Komter (1982), who studied a different type of side sequences as they occur in job interviews. She analyzed the problem how the interview is resumed after, for example, somebody has entered and left the room again.

11 It may be disputed whether this is a pre-self-invitation or just a first element of an indirect proposal, since it does not seem to ask 'what are you up to tonight', but 'will you be home tonight (and if so, I'll come round'), to which inquiry the second utterance is an account.

12 However, as Heritage (1984a:270) discusses, empirical research shows preferred responses tend to be accounted for (see note 13).

13 Drew (1984) shows how rejections of invitations tend to be formulated as an appreciation, followed by a rejection, and an explanation of the inability to accept the invitation. Rejections of invitations thus are built as [appreciation] + [rejection] + [account]. See also Heritage (1984a:270-1) on how recipients tend to refer to their inability rather than their unwillingness to respond to an initial action in the preferred way. Offers may be rejected with a claim of lack of need, or questions may be left

unanswered because recipient claims not to have knowledge. See also Levinson (1983) on the claim of inability to comply with requests.

14 Compare invitation-acceptance sequences as "come and see me some time" -"yes I will", whereas both parties know that the recipient does not know the speaker's address, and without the address being given or asked for.

15 It needs to be noted however, that not only does the invited party show little eagerness to come to the party, but the inviter may be seen as not being very convinced that J. should come round. J. is "quite wellcome" if she feels like coming. This sounds not very inviting. And most of all inviter's "Suit yourself" suggests that the success of the party does not depend on J.'s presence.

16 Schegloff & Sacks (1973) speak of an 'offer' instead of a 'proposal' for closing.

17 It is interesting to see how the doctor in the next fragment stopped the recording of the conversation after his "That's a deal then.". Apparently the arrival of an agreement about the therapy constitutes the end of the medical interview.

[LvdS: medical interview]
D. If it uh does not really work after
   uh five or six days or so, (...) then
   you've got to come back.=
P. =Ja:.=
D. =Ja?=
P. =Ja.=
D. That's a deal then.
   ((end of recording))

18 Diek van Bijsterveld brought this to my attention.

19 It may well be that a relationship exists between the length of the conversation and/or the social relationship between the participants on the one hand, and the length of the closing section on the other. The closing section seems not only to be used for closing down the conversation, but also for doing relation work in the same way as the opening section is used both for opening and relation work (cf. Ten Have, 1980, on relation work in opening sections).

20 The fact that this fragment lacks a second "bye bye", may be explained by the fact that it is speaker M. who controls the buttons of the tape-recorder. He seems to have pushed the 'Off' switch right after his own last utterance.

21 Sequences which started off as five-part structures may also be truncated after the fourth-positioned confirmation-utterance, for example:

[HH:TC:31:5]
M. ((extended piece of advice))
P. °Ja ja ja.°
M. Ja:?
P. Ja.
→ P. One more question.(...)

[HH:TC:15:11]
((after M has asked whether he could come by))
V. What time will you be coming then?
M. (Oh I don't know. I think) I'll drop
in on Mies'.
(0.7)
V. O:h ja:. That's alright as well.
M. Ja:?
V. Ja:h.
→ V. We're going to move now.

[HH:TC:5:13]
H. I would like it very much if you came as well.
P. Oh how nice.
(...)
H. Ja::?
P. Ja. That's nice. I'll write it down.
→ P. How's Wilfred doing?

22 Other terms used are 'off-topic markers' (Sacks S' 1971 April 9:8), 'touched-off utterances' (Sacks, April 4, 1968), and 'misplacement markers' (Schegloff & Sacks 1973:258).

23 It may be noted here that in Dutch word-order a disjunct marker does not need to be put into the first position of the utterance, although it may the case. In the first two examples there is a utterance-initial disjunct marker:
"Hey listen Martijn, something else, (...)"
"Furthermore I've (.) more or less promised (...)"
In the following examples, given in Dutch, the disjunct markers are inserted in the course of the

utterance. The markers are underlined:

"Ik heb trouwens een ( ) heb ik binnen."

"Maar hoe heeft u het trouwens geha:d?"

Striking however is that they do occur rather early in the utterance. When disjunct markers such as "trouwens", "overigens", or "verder" do occur in utterance-initial position, they tend to occur as parentheticals.

Transcription key

Apart from some minor deviations, the transcript notation used here has been developed by Gail Jefferson.

[[	Indicates the starting point of overlapping talk, for example, A. And honestly speaking ye:s [indeed. B. [Yes. The left-hand bracket is also used to indicate simultaneously starting talk, e.g., A. [=And honestly speaking ye:s indeed. B. [=Yes.
= =	Equal signs, one at the end of one line and one at the beginning of the next speaker's line, indicate no 'gap between the two lines', for example, A. And honestly speaking ye:s indeed.= B. =Yes.
(0.6)	Indicates a pause of 0.6 of a second.
(.)	Indicates a pause, smaller than 0.3 of a second.
w<u>o</u>rd	Underscoring indicates some form of stress, via pitch and/or amplitude.
:, ::	Colons indicate prolongation of the immediately preceding sound. The length of the colon row indicates the lenght of the prolongation.
, . ? ?	Punctuation markers indicate intonation as in written language.
.	A period indicates a stopping fall in tone, not necessarily the end of a sentence.
,	A comma indicates a continuing intonation.
?	A question mark indicates a rising intonation, not necessarily a question.

?	A combined question mark/comma indicates a rising intonation, weaker than that indicated by a question mark.
-	A dash indicates a halting or abrupt cutoff in a word or string of words.
° word°	The word(s) between degree signs is/are produced in a low voice. The more degree signs, the quieter the tone of voice is
WORD	Capital letters indicate that a word or string of words is spoken louder than the surrounding talk.
> word < < word >	When part of an utterance is delivered at a pace quicker or slower than the surrounding talk, it is indicated by being enclosed between > < or < > respectively.
.h .hh	Audible intake of breath.
(h)	An "(h)" inserted in a part of an utterance indicates that this part is produced laughingly.
( )	Empty single parentheses indicate that some part of the ongoing talk has not been understood by the transcriber.
(word)	A word between single parentheses indicates dubious hearing of this word by transcriber.
((coughs))	Double parentheses are used to enclose a description of some phenomenon, or commentary of the transcriber.
(...)	Three dots enclosed in single parentheses indicates that a part of the utterance has been left out.
HH:TC HH:FtF	These codes identify the fragments as belonging to Hanneke Houtkoop (HH) and as part of a telephone call (TC) or of a face-to-face conversation (FtF).

Dutch transcriptions of the data

CHAPTER 1

1. V. Wacht even. Ik doe de TV zachter, want ik
versta je moeilijk. (Moet hier namelijk
voetballen) kijken.

2. V. Eén moment Reina. Dag jonge. Komt een kind
van me binnen.

3. V. Hoe is het,
R. Nou prima:.
V. Ja:?
R. Ik ga even zitten. Hoeplakee. Zo.

CHAPTER 3

6. M. Ik denk dat 't ongelooflijk, ongehoorde
zware baan is.
(1.0)
P. Wat zeg je? Dat 't een?
M. Een ongehoord zware baan is.
P. Nou: leuk wel. [Denk ik.
M. [Jawel, heel leuk, maar eh
met e:norm veel haken en ogen.

18. T. Hoe oud ben je?
A. Nou eh>'k ben nog geen dertig<.
(.)
A. Hoor.
(0.9)
A. Dus.
(1.0)
T. Gh(h). Hoe- hoe oud wel?
A. Hahahaha.
A. I(h)k be(h)n no(h)g geen de(h)rtig. Ga-ha:.
Nee i(h)k be(h)n ne(h)genentwi(h)ntig.=
T. =Je zit niet voor de teevee.
(1.7)
T. Interview dit.

24. K. Met e:h Kees Koster.
    H. Da:g Kees.
    K. Lag je al in bed jonge?
    H. Nee hoor.
    K. O(h)o(h).

26. A. Ja, met Ageeth Snabel?
    (0.4)
    T. Da:g, met Ton, Ageeth.
    A. Ja hallo.
    T. Hallo.
    T. Zitten jullie op het balkon?
    (0.4)
    A. .hh Nee:, we zitten e:h naar de televisie te kijken.
    T. Och god.
    T. Wat is t'r?
    (0.3)
    A. .hh Ni(h)iks. Journaa:l.
    T. Oh, 't journaal. O:h.
    T. Kun je 't missen?=
    A. =.hh Ja nee we worden een dagje ouder. Nee eh ik kan 't wel missen. Ja hoor.
    T. Oh.
    T. Jullie zijn weer e::h terug van vakantie?

27. see 50

28. A. Moet ik t'r even roepen?
    C. Ja:, als eh (.) als 't kan graag, ja.=
    A. =Okay.

29. B. Moet je dan niet confirmeren.
    A. Nee:, prima.
    (0.5)
    B. O:kay:.

30. F. Hé, kom je ook?
    M. Waar?
    F. Hier?
    M. Oh dat is prima.
    (0.7)
    M. Nee, wat ik eigenlijk wilde weten, omdat eh- is Elly daar?

34. A. Met Catherijne?
    (0.7)
    C. Met Martijn.
    (0.5)

A. Hoi.=
C. =Hoi.

35. S. Martijn, tot kijk.
M. Okay::.
S. [Hoi:.
M. [Hoi:.

37. A. Ja hallo:.
C. Hallo: met e:h Ronny. Waldman.
(1.0)
C. Van Staalstraat nummer 47.
(1.0)
C. Met wie spreek ik? Met u:h
A. U:h met Patricia:. Jan en e:h Marijke zijn d'r niet.

43. see 69

44. see 6

49. see 136

CHAPTER 4

50. M. Mag ik Aletta dan even?
(0.3)
T. Ja:.
M. Okay:.
T. ALETTA:, JE MOEDER.

51. P. Mag ik m'n moe:der eve:?=
L. =(hi) J:a: hoor. Ik zal u eve:: (.) haar geve:n.=
P. =Ja.

52. R. Mag ik die heel eventjes?
J. Ik ga d'r even roepen. [Momentje graag.
R. [Okay. Beda:nkt.

53. R. Is jouw vrouw aanwezig?
J. Die is aanwezig ja:.
R. Mag ik die heel eventjes?

54. R. Is jouw moeder thuis?
D. Nee:.
R. Is jouw moeder niet thui:s?

55. R. Is jouw moeder thuis?
    M. Nee. Die is op d'r werk.
    R. Is die op d'r werk.

56. H. Is Annet in de buurt?=
    G. =Ja hoor.=
    H. =Okay.

57. B. Met Bonnie.
    P. Ja. Goedemiddag. U spreekt met Van der Broeck. Ik wilde vanmiddag even langskomen. Maar ik wilde even weten of u: e:h of ie d'r was.
    B. E::h nou:: hij is net weg. E:n met anderhalf uur zou die weer hier zijn. Dus om drie uur ongeveer.

58. see 131

59. M. Ik zal tegen d'r zeggen. Dat ze morgen die plaat van Fame even mee wil nemen.
    L. O:kay.
    M. Ja?
    L. Ja.
    M. Joe:.

60. H. Hoe laat kan ik komen?
    R. Eh (.) zeg maar (.) tien uur ongeveer?
    H. Ja prima.
    R. Ja?
    H. Doe ik dat.
    R. Okay.

61. R. Moet je luisteren, als je moeder nou thui:skomt,
    D. Ja:.
    R. zeg maar even dat ik haar behel, omdat Marce:l vanavond e:h dus eh niet op judo wil.
    D. Ja:?
    R. Zou je dat eventjes tegen je moeder willen zeggen?
    D. Ja.
    R. Maar dan bel ik 'r nog wel voor zes uur.
    D. Ja.
    R. Zeg dat maar tegen d'r.
    D. Ja.
    R. Ja?
    D. Da::g.
    R. Okay::.
    R. Da:g Duncan.

62. V. Ja. 'T gaat maar door joh.
    P. Gelukkig wel.
    V. Ja, ken 't niet begrijpen, maar 't is zo.

P. Ja:, gelukkig wel man.

63. K. Zo'n (.) prima heerlijk fietsje.=
P. =Ja::, da's zeker een lekker fietsje.

64. A. Eh ik Roy, die heeft e:::h vandaag ziek
gemeld, omdat hij aanrijding gehad heeft.=
I. =Is 't- Ja?
A. Ja.

65. K. Hoe is het verder?
P. Goed wel.
K. Ja?=
P. =Ja: 's wel goed.
(0.7)
P. Wel goed. Redelijk aardig.

66. D. Maar laa'k zo zeggen, .h als ik denk van
ik zellef wel e:h de puf om e:h te klussen,
ik (bel even) op.
(0.9)
P. Ja.
(0.3)
D. Dan e:h dan geef ik je eventueel een seintje.=
P. =Doe dat maar.

67. P. Zal ik Lodewijk dan eventjes be:lle:n?=
S. =Ja:::.
(0.7)
P. En dan (.) e:::::h::m bel ik jou weer op
wat we doe:n.
S. Ja. Pri:ma.
P. Ja?

68. S. Maar (.) echt, als je samen bent zou ik zou
'k dat niet doen hoor.
H. Nee.
S. Want dat is echt een knoets van een boerderij.
H. Nee: maar dat heb 'k ook niet zoveel behoefte
aan verder.

69. M. Zeg maar tegen Hans,
(0.6)
K. Ja.
M. als- als hij thuis terugkomt, voor twalef
uur vannacht, dan moet hij me even bellen.
(0.6)
K. Ja.
(0.3)
M. Je weet wie ik ben hê?

K. ((zucht diep))
M. Of niet? Ja::. Martijn uit Rotterdam. Je
bent een keer bij me op bezoek geweest.
((gekraak))
K. Ja.
M. Ja?

70. A. 'K wou vragen of e:h jullie de sleutel
die je van mijn huis hebt,
(.)
R. Ja:.
A. van bene:den,
(0.6)
A. in een envelop wil doen, en bij A:ns (.)
wil afgeven. In de Hartstraat.
(1.3)
R. O:h.
A. As dat kan.
((enkele regels overgeslagen))
A. .hh Want Ans die komt hier eh logeren
als wij op vakantie gaan.
(.)
R. O::h ja:. Nou pri:ma.

71. see 136

72. V. Nou. Dan weten we genoeg. Dan e::h (.)
[want dan ken ik Margreet bellen, zie je.
R. [z- za-
(1.0)
R. Ja::.
((enkele regels overgeslagen))
V. =Heel kort. Ja:. Want ik moet Margreet nog
bellen joh. Die zit er op te wachten.
(0.6)
R. Ja:.
(.)
R. O:h vand[aar.
V. [Hè:?

73. B. E:::h dan moet ze: (1.0) voor e:h tien
uur opbellen.
R. Voor tien uur.
B. Om tie:n uur eh moet ik weg.
R. Oh ja. Doe:n we:.

74. see 75

75. S. Dan zou 't voor ons erg plezierig zijn
om aan te sluiten bij zeven juli.

H. Juli.=
S. =Ja. Dus aan te sluiten tot.=
H. =Ja ja. Oh ja. Tot.
S. En daarvoor.

76. see 117

78. A. Sorry Ron, ((geeuwend:)) ik ga m'n tanden
poetsen, ((geeuwt luid)) en ik ga naar bed.
(2.1)
A. 'K ben moe:.
(1.7)
A. Van alles. Van het le:ven.
(1.8)
R. Ja. Dat komt mooi ui:t. Wa' je gaat volgende
week op vakantie.

79. see 83

80. R. 'K zal wel even overleggen, maa::r da:n krij' je
dus die situatie dat Marion 't op woensdag wi:l,
(1.2)
R. Omdat zij naar Herman wil.

81. see 117

82. see 70

83. R. Is:: Ne:l ook aanwezig?
H. E::h bel je over vijf minuten even terug?
R. Zeg je:?=
H. =Bel je over vijf minuten even terug?
(0.8)
H. Dan is ze d'r.
R. Oh ja. Doe: ik.

84. K. Is dokter Van Veen misschien aanwezig?=
V. =Nee helaas niet. Die is misschien met vakantie.

85. R. I:s jouw moeder thui:s?
M. Nee. Die is op d'r werk.

86. R. Is je moeder daar?
J. Nee:. Die is e:h voor 't buurtkrantje (   )

87. H. Is de assistente d'r?
T. Nee die is ziek.

88. K. .hh Ik was eigenlijk op zoek naar de heer
Koopman.

(0.7)
D. E::h die is vrij.

89. L. Hé dan heb ik een ander vraagje:,
R. Ja:.
L. e:h ik zit 'n beetje met 'n moeilijkheid,
ik moet een was draaien,
R. Ja:.
L. en ik kan eigenlijk niet de deur uit, want (.)
ik heb me ziek gemeld, (.) en ik vin 't een
beetje link om (.) de straat over te gaan.
R. Ja:.
L. Dus ik wilde vragen of ik misschien een wasje
bij jou kon draaien.

90. see 148

91. see 117

92. see 69

93. see 136

94. M. Ik kom morgen even langs.
(0.9)
M. Tegen 'n-[
F. [Ja nee prima.
M. tegen een uur of half zes.

95. see 67

96. see 125

97. R. (Ook) leuk om 't met z'n drieën te doen.
A. Ja:.
R. Eerlijk gezegd.

98. A. 'K ga nu naar be:d.
(.)
R. Ja:.
A. Lijkt me hee:rlijk. Om naar bed te gaan.

99. see 130

100 M. Dan stuur ik 'm gelijk door naar jou.
(.)
F. Ja.
(0.4)
F. Hartstikke goed.
M. Ja?

101 see 60

102 see 121

103 see 125

104 F. Hé, kom je ook?
M. Waar?
F. Hier?
M. Oh da's prima.

105 M. Oh ik zou:: mo:rgenmi:dda:g ku:nne:n, vrijdag-
middag tussen dus kunnen vanaf: half een.
(0.9)
P. Tot?
(0.6)
M. Tot een uur of (2.6) ze:ven, (.) ha:lf a:cht.
(0.9)
P. Ja, laten we dat maar doen.

107 B. Wil je tegen al onze (pierewarrige) bestuurs-
leden zeggen dat 'k er: (.) niet bij kan zijn?
A. Potverdo:mme.
B. ((lacht))
A. Ja. Ik zal 't even zeggen.

108 see 57

109 M. Hé (.) luister 's.
B. Ja(h).
M. Wat doe jij vanavond met Margreet? Want
ik heb jullie huis helemaal niet gezien.
B. Nou: als je 't wil zien (.) wij gaan
vanavond inpakken.
M. Nou: dan kom ik vanavond even langs.

111 A. Misschien kunnen we dan met z'n vieren gaan.=
M. =Oh prima.
M. En ze bloosde diep rood achter de oren. Mary.
(0.9)
A. Nou ze is er niet.
M. Nee maa:r nu wel. Straks wel. Toen je dat vroeg.
A. °hahahaha°.
M. Mary, i- i- ik moet je wat vragen. Iets heel
persoonlijks.
A. [Hohohohhahahahah. Wil je met me naaien? Hahaha.
M. [Pom-pom-pom ((zingend)). ( )
A. Ik wil je wat persoonlijks vragen. Wil je met me
naar bed. [Hahahahahaha.

M. [Hohohohohoho. Nou .hh [Nou maar goed.
A. [Ah hum. Ja.
M. Ik vind het 'n prima idee, (...)

112 see 144

113 K. Als ik ze wil hebben, kom ik ze wel even ophaːlen.
(0.8)
M. Hoe laat ongeveer?
K. Of ben jij e:ten en zo?
M. Ik ga tegen 'n uur of zes eten.
K. Ja.
(1.5)
K. °hm::::::::° Even [zien, hoe laat is het nu?
M. [Kwart voor ( )
K. Kwart voor zes.
M. Ja.
K. .hh E::h nou. Als ik ze wil hebben, kom ik voor zessen langs.
((enkele regels overgeslagen))
M. O:kay.

114 see 105

115 B. U kunt naar het advokatenkantoor gaan,
(0.7)
B. dat is vanavond,
P. Ja:.
B. en u kunt even bellen (.) eh voor een telefonisch advies met de rechtshulp van de Vrije Universiteit.
P. O:h. Weet u dat nummer?=

116 M. Met Martij:n.
P. Hé dag Martijn, met Pe:ter.
M. Dag > Martijn met Peter <. E:hm ja?
P. E:h kun jij morgen in plaats van: e:h eén uur om::: twee uur half drie komen?
(4.5)
M. Ja: hoo:r.
M. Dat moet toch? ((zacht lachend:)) Ik kan niet anders hè?
P. Nou ja:, ik vraag het maa:r.
(0.3)
P. As je zegt van nou ja "mm-mm-mm".=
M. =Redden we 't dan?
P. .hh Je had tot e::h hoe laat de tij:d? Zeven uur?
(0.3)
M. Nee hoo:r. Ik heb tot e:h a:cht=
P. =Ja:, dan redden we 't.=

M. =>acht uur de tijd<. Ja?
P. Ja.
(0.4)
M. 'K ben om twee uur bij je.
(0.6)
P. O:kay:.=
M. =Ja:?=
P. =Ja, doe:n we:.=
M. =Tot mo:rgen.=
P. [=Bye:.
M. [=Doe::.

117 G. Gerard.
M. (Ja.)
M. Met Martijn.=
M. =Een afspraakje.
G. Ja.
M. Kan dat? Donderdagmiddag.
(1.1)
M. Of ben ik dan te laat?
G. <Donderdagmiddag? >
((enkele regels overgeslagen))
G. E::::hm (2.0) [Ja dat kan wel.
M. [( )
(.)
G. Donderdag. ((hardop schrijvend?))
(1.1)
G. Nee. Wacht even.
G. ((gemompel))
M. Vrijdag is ook prima.
G. Vrijdag is ook prima.
(.)
G. Even nadenken.
(2.0)
M. Tenminste (.) vrijdagmorgen niet, (ik ben
donderdagmiddag we:l in principe)
G. Nou doe maar donderdagmiddag.=
M. =Ja?
G. Ja.

118 see 107

119 R. Zou je dat eventjes tegen je moeder willen zeggen?

120 K. Maar wil jij dat doen?

121 K. Maar wil jij dat doen?
(0.6)
Z. Ja:. (.) Tuurlijk.
K. Ja?

(1.1)
Z. Kan die gewoon met een e:h (apparaat). Of wa:t?=
K. =Wee:t ik vee:l? Het is een Philips.
Z. Ja.
(2.6)
Z. Ja. (Da' wil 'k wel even [doen.)
K. [Ja?
Z. ( ) demonteren ja.
K. Okay.

122 R. Misschien wil je aan haar vragen of ze mij: even be:lt?
(0.3)
H. Ja:. Dat kan ik doen.=
H. =Wa's je numm[er?
R. ['T is wel dringend.=
R. =In Amsterda:m, zes acht nul,[twee negen acht.
H. [°Wacht even hoor°.
H. Ze:s.=
R. =acht nu:l,=
H. =Zes acht nu:l,=
R. =Ja:. Twee negen acht.=
H. =Twee negen >acht<.
(0.8)
H. Ja. Nee:. Ze zal zo wel komen.
R. Ja:?
H. Ja. Okay.=
R. =Bedankt.=
H. =Hoi.

123 see 132

124 M. Wil je vragen of ie mij wil bellen?
V. Of tie jou wil bellen?
M. Ja?
V. O:kay.
(.)
V. Martij:n hè?
M. Martij:n, in Rotterdam.
V. In Rotterdam.
V. [O:kay.
M. [Ja?=
M. =Dank je we:l.
M. Da:g.
((einde opname))

125 C. .hh Die mag je dus uit die kartonnen doosjes halen, (.) en in een houten kistje verpakken.
A. Ja:: tuurlijk.
C. Ja?

A. Ja.
C. <Wil je dat zo snel mogelijk doen? >
(0.9)
C. En mij dan even laten weten wanneer dat klaar is?
A. Ja: okay.
C. Ja?
A. Ik heb trouwens een ((merknaam)) heb ik binnen.
C. O::h dat is maar 'n hee:l klein dingetje: (...)

126 M. E::hm is- zou jij eventueel morgen
naar 't Lingehuis kunnen komen?
P. Ja: da's goed.=
M. =Kan dat?
P. Ja hoor.
M. E::hm maakt' voor jou nog wat uit? Is-is-is
zou half twaalf kunnen?
(1.0)
P. E:h ja. Dan ben ik er wel hoor.
M. Ja?=
P. =Ja, dan ben 'k er al lang. Ja.=
M. =Oh. Dus je zit er sowieso al.=
((enkele regels overgeslagen))
M. Nou, zullen we (.) half (.) twaalf zeggen?
Precies.=
M. [=Lijkt mij 't beste.
P. [=Dat lijkt me beter. In de kantine.=
M. [=Ja:?
P. [=Ja:, dat is goed.
M. Dan e:h zorg ik echt dat ik gewoon dan d'r ben.
P. En dan heb ik die boeken bij: me:,=
M. [=Ja?
P. [=Uitstekend.
P. En dan e::h kunnen we nog even babbelen.=
M. =Ja. Okay:.
P. [Ja?
M. [Goed zo.
M. Zie 'k je morgen.=
P. =Tot morgen.=
M. =Joe:oe:.
P. [Da:g.
M. [Bedankt. Da::g.

127 I. Goedemo:rgen.
D. Goedemorgen.
I. Eh-[
D. [Ed van Werkvo:ge:l.
I. Ja. Met Ireen Bank.
I. Ik wilde ee:n afspraak ma:ken met (dokter)
D. Dat zal wel gaan.
D. Wanneer wil je komen?

I. E::h (   ) is er vandaag nog een plaatsje?
D. Ja hoor.
I. Ja?
D. Ja.
D. Half twaalf?
I. Pri:ma:.=
D. =O[kay.
I. [En (.) mijn vriend wil ook komen.=
D. =En je vriend ook?
I. Ja:.=
D. =Nou, die kan dan om twaalf uur. Mag dat?=
I. =Ja. Prima:.=
D. =Goed zo:.=
D. =Hoe heet ie?
I. E::h Ireen en Peter.
D. Hahahahahah. Je moest e(h)ven de(h)nken.
(.)
D. Ire:ne, haha.
(.)
D. Hoe die heette.
I. ('K denk heb nou) wel de goeie.
D. Hahahahah[ha.
I. [Haha.=
D. =Ja. Haha. Okay. Peter breng je dus mee?
I. Ja. [Goe::d.
D. [Tot zo:. Tot kijk.
D. [Da:g.
I. [Da:g.

130 G. Maar bemoei je niet met die meiden en hou je bij je vriendin en eh (.) bek ze maar af.
C. Jha.
G. Hè?
G. [Want 't is echt eh (.) onzin (.) onzin onzin.
C. [Ja.
C. Dus ik kan 't gewoon aanhouden met hem?
G. Ja joh natuurlijk. (.) Tuurlijk.

131 F. Maar kom hier naar toe, dan kunnen we 't er allemaal even rustig over hebben.=
M. =Prima.
(0.5)
F. Ja?=
M. =Ik kom zo (even) bij je langs.=
F. =O:kay. Tot zo.=
M. =Ma:zzel.

132 H. Dan zou ik het leuk vinden als jij ook kwam.
K. Oh leu:k zeg.
K. Op zes mei?

H. Ja. 's Middags om een uur of drie.
K. 's Middags om een uur of drie.
H. Ja::?
K. Ja. Vin ik leuk. Zal ik even opschrijven.
K. H-a-r-r-i-ë-t j-a-r-i-g.

133 H. ((uitnodiging)
A. O:h wat gezellig.
H. Dat lijkt me ook.
A. Ja:.
H. Kom je ook?
A. Ja:.
H. Heel leuk.
A. Zondag.
H. Zondag ja.
A. Ik zal 't meteen even opschrijven.

134 H. Hé moet je horen. Ik bel nog even wat mensen op.
A. Ja:.
H. Dan zie ik je zondag.
A. Ja.
H. Ja?
A. Ja: [okay.
H.   [Om een uur of drie.
A. Ja, ik heb het opgeschreven.
H. O::kay.

135 H. Goed hé Kees. Zie ik je zondag.
K. Ja okay Harriët.

136 H. E:::h moet je luisteren, zondag om een uur of
drie dan is er een borrel hier. Want eh ik ben
van de week jarig, dus als je zin hebt om te
komen ben je van harte welkom.
J. Oh.
H. En Jan ook.
J. Nou dank je wel.
H. Ja?
J. [Uur of drie.
H. [Moet je maar kijken.
J. Ik zal het onthouden.
H. Zondag uur of drie, ja?

137 M. Dan zou je 'm vrijdagmorgen op moeten vangen even.
F. A::h geen probleem joh.
M. Geen probleem?
F. Nee:hee:. Geen enkel probleem.=
M. =Ik ga 'm gelijk bellen.
F. Okay.
M. Ma:zzel.

138 M. Hé Klaas, zal ik afspreken zaterdag rond elf uur?
K. (Prima)
M. Hja?
K. Okay.
M. Ik zie je dan.
K. Goed zo.=
M. [=Mazze:l.
K. [=Okay.
M. Doe:i.
K. (   )

139 see 116

140 M. Da:n e:h kan ik 'm wel naar jou doorsturen?
F. Ja natuurlijk.
(0.7)
M. Okay.
F. Natuurlijk.
F. Da:n zorg ik d'r voor dat ik dat regel.
(0.6)
M. Oh prima.
F. Ja?

142 A. En dan wil ik graag dat als die kuur op is,
(0.7)
A. dat u even ik elk geval contact opneemt, (...)
P. Ja ja [   )=
A. [=Ja?
P. [=Bedankt in ie[der geval.
A. [Afgesproken hoor.=
P. =(Da:g).
(.)
A. Da:g (mevrouw).
((einde opname))

143 R. Nou moet je luisteren,
K. Ja.
R. zeg dan eventjes tegen d'r as je d'r no:g
vōor die tijd eh ziet, hahahaha.
K. Ja:.
R. (...) dat ze dan in ieder geval voor vrijdag
even be:lt,
K. Ja.
R. om even 'n afspraakje te maken.
K. Okay.
R. Ja:?=
K. =Ja.=
R. =Okay:.=
K. =Ōk[ay.
R. [Hé tot ziens hè.=

K. =D[oe:.
R. [Doe:.

144 H. Hoe laat kan ik komen?
T. Eh (.) zeg maar (.) tien uur ongeveer?
H. Ja prima
T. Ja?
H. Doe ik dat.
T. Ok[ay
H. [Okay. Bedankt.
T. [Da:g
H. [Da:g

145 H. Twee vijf drie.
(.)
H. Ik bel hem even op.
M. O:kay.
H. Okay. Bedankt.
M. Doei:.
((einde opname))

146 M. Twee drie acht.
B. Ja. Dat is 't.
M. Ik e:h ga hun proberen te bereiken.
B. Heel graag.
M. Okay:.
B. Bedankt
(.)
B. Da:g
((einde opname))

147 D. Ik za:l 't laten kijken.
(.)
D. Kunt u altijd eventueel e:h stra:ks
nog opbellen.=
M. =Okay.=
D. =Ja?
D. [Prima:.
M. [Bedankt.
M. Da:g.=
D. =Da:g meneer

148 P. Ik eh eh ik bel je even terug, want de telefoon
staat beneden >boven<, en het eh die is beneden.
Wij hebben maar een toestel en die staat naast
het bed en het adres ligt beneden.
H. [Ja.
P. [Bel 'k je zo even terug.=
H. =O:kay.=
P. =Ja?=

H. =Tot zo dan.=
P. =Tot zo.=
H. [=Bedankt.
P. [=Doe:g

149 M. Okay.=
D. =Ja?
M. Bedankt.

150 M. Okay.=
D. =Ja?
M. [Bedankt.
D. [Prima:.

151 V. [Okay:.
M. [Ja?=
M. =Dank je we:l.
M. Da:g.
((einde opname))

152 M. Ik kom naar jou.
G. O:kay.=
M. =Ja?
M. [Da:g.
G. [Tot dan.
G. Da::g.

153 M. Je hoort vanmiddag nog van mij.
A. Ja:.
M. Ja[:?
A. [Prima.
M. Ma:zze:l.=
A. =Zeg, doe:g.
M. Doei::.

154 see 125

155 R. Ik zal 't doorgeven joh.=
S. =Ja.=
R. =Ja?
S. Ve:rde:r had ik (.) min of meer beloofd e::::h

156 M. Dan kom ik op jouw fiets,
(0.9)
V. Ja::.=
M. =en dan neem ik de auto mee terug.
(0.3)
V. O:h, da's ook prima.
M. Ja:?
(1.5)

V. Wij:: e::h:::m zagen Ysbrand is nog even hier,

FOOTNOTES TO CHAPTER 4

(1) R. Hé, en is e:h Ronnie d'r ook?=
A. =Nee:.
R. O:ho:h.
A. Hu(h).
R. Hu(h). Ben j'alleen?=
A. =Nee: ja:. Bedoel ik.
R. Nee ja(h).
A. Ha(h)uh. Die is in de gara:ge. Dus ik voel me niet echt alleen?=
R. =O:h.=
A. =Want hij zit om de hoek.
(0.7)
R. O:h ja.
(0.7)
A. Maar waarom bel je dan?

M. E:h Ireen is t'r zeker niet.
P. Ja, die is t'r wel.=
M. =O:h [ja:.
P. [Die is t'r wel.=
M. =Nee goed.
P. Moet ik t'r even roepen?
M. Ja: als eh (.) als 't kan graag, ja.=
P. =Okay.

(2) L. Is e:h Mariëtte nog op?
M. Ja: die zit in bad.
(0.8)
L. O(h)och.

C. Is dokter Marijnsen aanwezig?
A. Die is in vergadering.
C. Oh.

(5) A. Maar je leert er altijd wel iets van hè?
(0.5)
R. Ja: ik loop die cursus nou ook eh zelf,=
A. =Ja.
R. al e:h (0.8) sinds eh september,
A. Ja:.
R. 't is haast afgelopen en=
A. =Ja ja.
R. en over een maandje is de laatste lezing dan

e::h moet ik ook e:h sprekend=
A. =Ja:.
R. nee e:h vloeiend leren spreken.

(6) see 61

(7) E. Je weet dat je morgen moet eh voetballen?
Tenminste [dat er voetballen is.
R. [Ik weet dat ik moet.
R. Ja. Ik doe ook mee.
E. Je weet ook waar?
R. E:h in e:h Sloten hè?
E. Sloterdijk, ja.
(0.7)
E. Weet je [waar 't is?
R. [Hoe ga jij, ga jij met de auto?
E. Ja, ik ga heel vroeg, ik heb wel een auto, maar ik ga (.) om e:h tien uur al weg. Want ik moet eerst ergens eh langs.=
R. =Oh ja. Dan ga ik anders.
((enkele regels overgeslagen))
E. Maar als je dan met de bus gaat, dan kan je wel e:h mee terug rijden.
R. Oh ja, da's prima. Ja. Graag.

(17)A. Lukt 't eh nie voldoende na: zeg maar> 'n dag of < vijf zes, (...) dan moe' je even terugkomen.=
P. =Ja:.=
A. =Ja?=
P. =Ja.=
A. =Afgesproken.

(21)M. ((uitgebreid advies))
P. °Ja ja ja°
M. Ja:?
P. Ja.
P. Nog een vraagje. (...)

V. Hoe laat kom je dan?
M. (Oh dat weet ik niet. Ik denk) da'k even langs Mies ga.
(0.7)
V. O:h ja:. Kan ook.
M. Ja:?
V. Ja:h.
V. We gaan nu verhuizen.

H. Ik zou het heel leuk vinden als je ook kwam.
P. Oh leu:k zeg.
((enkele regels overgeslagen))
H. Ja::?
P. Ja. Lijkt me leuk. Ik schrijf het op.
P. Hoe gaat het met Wilfred?

CHAPTER 5

157 see 24

158 see 24

159 see 56

160 see 161

161 O. Is Henk Brandon d'r ook?
(.)
A. Ja, die zit hier.
A. Een ogenblikje asublief.

162 see 131

163 see 100

164 see 75

165 see 117

166 see 82

167 see 89

168 see 130

169 see 121

170 see 121

171 see 122

172 see 131

173 see 131

174 see 134

175 see 116

176 see 152

Bibliography

ALEXANDER, J. ET AL. (forthcoming). The micro-macro link. University of California Press: Berkeley and Los Angeles

APPEL, R., G. HUBERS & G. MEYER. 1976. Sociolinguistiek. Utrecht,Antwerpen: Spectrum

ATKINSON,J.M. 1982. 'Understanding formality: the categorization and production of 'formal' interaction.' In: The British Journal of Sociology 33, 1, 1982, 86-117

ATKINSON, J.M. & P. DREW. 1979. Order in Court. The organisation of verbal interaction in judicial settings. London: McMillan

ATKINSON, J.M. & J. HERITAGE (Eds.). 1984. Structures of social action. Studies in conversation analysis. Cambridge: Cambridge University Press

AUSTIN, J.L. 1962. How to do things with words. Oxford: Oxford University Press

BAR-HILLEL, Y. 1954. 'Indexical expressions.' In: Mind 63, 1954, 359-79

BEAUGRANDE, R. de & W. DRESSLER. 1981. Introduction to textlinguistics. London: Longman

BERGMANN, J.R. 1981. 'Ethnomethodologische Konversationsanalyse.' In: Schröder & Steger (eds.), 1981, 9-52

BLUM-KULKA, S. & E. OHLSTAIN. 1985. 'Requests and apologies: A cross-cultural study of speech act realization patterns (CCSARP).' In: Applied Linguistics 5, 196-213

BLUMER,H. 1966. 'Sociological implications of the thought of George Herbert Mead.' In: American Journal of Sociology 71, 1966, 535-544

BOLINGER, D. (Ed.). 1972. Intonation. Selected readings. Harmondsworth: Penguin

BROWN, G. & G. YULE. 1983. Discourse Analysis. Cambridge: Cambridge University Press

BUTTON, G. (forthcoming) 'Varieties of closings.' To appear in Psathas & Frankel (eds.)

BUTTON, G. & N. CASEY. 1984. 'Generating Topic: the use of topic initial elicitors.' In: Atkinson & Heritage (eds.), 1984, 167-190

CLARK, H.H. & J.W. FRENCH. 1981 'Telephone goodbyes.' In: Language in Society 10, 1, 1981, 1-19

COLE, P. & J.L. MORGAN (Eds.) 1975. Syntax and semantics,

vol.3: speech acts. New York: Academic Press
COULTHARD, M. 1977. An introduction to discourse analysis London: Longman
CRAMER, Y. 1985. Topic change: Van de hak op de tak spreken. Werkstuk, Katholieke Hogeschool Tilburg
DAVIDSON, J. 1984. 'Subsequent versions of invitations, offers, requests, and proposals dealing with potential or actual rejection.' In: Atkinson & Heritage (eds.), 1984, 102-128
DIK, S.C. & J.G. KOOIJ. 1979. Algemene Taalwetenschap. Utrecht: Spectrum
DIJK, T.A. van (Ed.) 1985. Handbook of discourse analysis. vol 3 Discourse and dialogue. New York: Academic Press
DOUGLAS, J.D. (Ed). 1971. Understanding everyday life. Toward the reconstruction of sociological knowledge. London: Routledge & Kegan Paul (Quoted from the 1973 edition)
DREW, P. 1984. 'Speakers' reportings in invitation sequences.' In: Atkinson & Heritage (eds.), 1984, 129-151
DRIESSEN, Ch. & H. van MIERLO, 1984. Problemen bij een functionele classificatie van 'nou'. Werkstuk Katholieke Hogeschool Tilburg
DRIESSEN, Ch. & H. van MIERLO (forthcoming). Afsluitingssequenties in nederlandse telefoongesprekken. Werkstuk Katholieke Universiteit Brabant
EDMONDSON, W. 1981. Spoken discourse: A model for analysis London, New York: Longman
EEMEREN, F.H. van & R. GROOTENDORST, 1982. 'The speech acts of arguing and convincing in externalized discussions.' In: Journal of Pragmatics 6, 1982, 1-24
EHLICH, K. 1979. 'Formen und Funktionen von "HM". Eine phonologisch-pragmatische Analyse.' In: Weydt (ed.), 503-517
ERVIN-TRIPP, S. 1981. 'How to make and understand a request.' In: Parret et al. (eds.), 1981, 195-209
FISHER, S. 1984. 'Institutional authority and the structure of discourse.' In: Discourse Processes 7, 201-224
FISHER, S. & A.D. TODD (Eds.). 1983. The social organization of doctor-patient communication. Washington DC: Center for Applied Linguistics
FOOLEN, A., J. HARDEVELD & D. SPRINGORUM (Eds.) 1980. Conversatie Analyse. Lezingen van het Congres CONVERSATIE ANALYSE gehouden op 17, 18 en 19 december 1979 in Nijmegen. Groningen: Xeno
FRANCK, D. 1979. 'Speech act and conversational move.' In: Journal of Pragmatics 3, 5, 1979, 461-467
FRANCK, D. 1980. Grammatik und Konversation. Königstein: Scriptor
FRANCK, D. 1984. 'Speaking about speech acts.' In: Journal of Pragmatics 8, 1, 1984, 87-92

FRANKEL, R.M. 1984. 'From sentence to sequence: understanding the medical encounter through microinteractional analysis.' In: Discourse Processes 7, 135-170
FRANKEL,R. (forthcoming). 'Talking in interviews: a dispreference for patient-initiated questions in physician-patient encounters.' To appear in Psathas & Frankel (eds.)
GARFINKEL, H. 1962. 'Common sense knowledge of social structures: the documentary method of interpretation in lay and professional fact finding.' In: J.M. Scher (ed.), 1962, Theories of the Mind. New York: Free Press of Glencoe. Republished in (and quoted from) Garfinkel, 1967a, 76-103
GARFINKEL, H. 1964. 'Studies in routine grounds of everyday activities.' In: Social Problems, 1964, Vol.11, 225-250. Republished in [and quoted from] Garfinkel, 1967a, 35-75
GARFINKEL, H. 1967a. Studies in ethnomethodology. Englewood Cliffs, NJ: Prentice-Hall
GARFINKEL, H. 1967b. 'What is ethnomethodology?' In: Garfinkel 1967a, 1-35
GARFINKEL, H. & H. SACKS. 1970. 'On formal structures of practical actions.' In: McKinney & Tiryakian (eds.), 338-366
GIBBS, R.W.Jr. 1981. 'Your wish is my command: convention and context in interpreting indirect requests.' In: Journal of Verbal Learning and Verbal Behavior 20, 1981, 431-444
GIBBS, R.W.Jr. 1986. 'What makes some indirect speech acts conventional?' In: Journal of Memory and Language 25, 181-196
GILS, M. van. 1985. Van uitstel komt afstel?? Onderzoek naar het verloop van afsluitingen van alledaagse telefoongesprekken. Werkstuk Katholieke Hogeschool Tilburg
GOFFMAN, E. 1967. Interaction ritual. Essays on face to face behavior. New York: Anchor Books
GOFFMAN, E. 1971. Relations in public. New York: Basic Books
GOFFMAN, E. 1976. 'Replies and responses.' In: Language and Society 5, 1976, 257-313. Republished in (and quoted from) Goffman, 1981, 5-78
GOFFMAN, E. 1981. Forms of talk. Philadelphia: University of Pennsylvania
GOODWIN,C. 1979. 'The interactive construction of a sentence in natural conversation.' In:Psathas (ed), 1979, 97-122
GOODWIN, C. 1981. Conversational organization:interaction between speakers and hearers. New York: Academic Press
GOODWIN,M.H. 1980. 'Processes of mutual monitoring implicated in the production of description sequences.' In:

Sociological Inquiry 50, 3/4, 1980, 303-317
GREATBATCH, D. 1985. The social organisation of news interview interaction. Department of Sociology, University of Warwick. Unpubl. Ph.D. dissertation
GREEN, G.M. 1975. 'How to get people to do things with words: the whimperative question.' In: Cole & Morgan (eds.), 1975, 107-143
GRICE, H.P. 1975. 'Logic and conversation.' In: Cole & Morgan (eds.), 1975, 41-58
GUMPERZ, J.J. 1982. 'The linguistic bases of communicative competence.' In: Tannen (ed.), 1982, 323-335
GUMPERZ, J.J. & D. **HYMES (Eds.)**. 1972. Directions in sociolinguistics. The ethnography of communication. New York: Holt,Rinehart & Winston
HANCHER, M. 1979. 'The classification of cooperative illocutionary acts.' In: Language in Society 8, 1, 1979, 1-14
HAVE, P. ten. 1977. 'Etnomethodologie.' In: Rademaker & Bergman (eds.), 1977, 145-168
HAVE, P. ten. 1980. 'Openingssequenties.' In: Foolen et al. (eds.). 1980, 63-84
HAVE, P. ten. 1986. Talk and institution: a reconsideration of the 'asymmetry' of doctor-patient interaction. Paper given at the Conference on Conversation Analysis and Ethnomethodology, University of California, Santa Barbara. March 26-29, 1986.
HAVERKATE, W.H. 1979. Impositive sentences in Spanish. Theory and description in linguistic pragmatics. Amsterdam etc.: North Holland Press
HERITAGE, J. 1984a. Garfinkel and ethnomethodology. Cambridge: Polity Press
HERITAGE, J. 1984b. 'A change-of-state token and aspects of its sequential placement.' In: Atkinson & Heritage (eds.), 1984, 299-345
HERITAGE, J. 1985. 'Analyzing news interviews:Aspects of the production of talk for an overhearing audience.' In: van Dijk (ed.), 1985, 95-117
HERITAGE, J. & J.M. **ATKINSON**. 1984. 'Introduction.' In: Atkinson & Heritage (eds.), 1984, 1-15.
HOUTKOOP-STEENSTRA, J.P. 1980. '"Je hebt wel gelijk, maar ...": Enige pragmatische aspecten van consessief-adversatieve "wel-maar"-constructies.' In: Publicaties van het Instituut voor Algemene Taalwetenschap 28, Amsterdam: Universiteit van Amsterdam
HOUTKOOP-STEENSTRA, H. 1986a. 'Eigenschappen van aangrenzende paren.' In: Gramma 10, 1, 1986, 1-24
HOUTKOOP-STEENSTRA, J.P. 1986b. Opening sequences in Dutch telephone conversations. Paper given at the Conference on Conversation Analysis and Ethnomethodology, University of California, Santa Barbara. March 26-29,

1986
HOUTKOOP-STEENSTRA, H. 1986c. 'Claimen en demonstreren in gesprekken.' In: Tijdschrift voor Taalbeheersing 8, 1986, 222-234
HOUTKOOP-STEENSTRA, H. & H. **MAZELAND**. 1982. 'Beurten en grotere gesprekseenheden.' In: Interdisciplinair Tijdschrift voor Taal- en Tekstwetenschap 2, 1982, 105-135
HOUTKOOP, H. & H. **MAZELAND**. 1985. 'Turns and discourse units in everyday conversation.' In: Journal of Pragmatics 9, 5, 1985, 595-619
HYMES, D.H. 1971. On communicative competence. Philadelphia: University of Pennsylvania. Partly republished in (and quoted from) Pride & Holmes (eds.), 1972, 269-293
JEFFERSON, G. 1972. 'Side sequences.' In: Sudnow (ed.), 294-338
JEFFERSON,G. 1973. 'A case of precision timing in ordinary conversation: Overlapped tag-positioned address terms in closing sequences.' In: Semiotica 9, 47-96
JEFFERSON, G. 1978a. 'Sequential aspects of story-telling in conversation.' In: Schenkein (ed.), 1978, 219-248
JEFFERSON, G. 1978b. At first I thought: A normalizing device for extraordinary events. (lecture)
JEFFERSON,G. 1979. 'A technique for inviting laughter and its subsequent acceptance/declination.' In: Psathas (ed.), 79-96
JEFFERSON,G. 1980a. 'On "trouble-premonitory" response to inquiry.' In: Sociological Inquiry 50, 3/4, 153-185
JEFFERSON, G. 1980b. Final report to the (British) SSRC on the analysis of conversations in whch "troubles" and "anxieties" are expressed Nr. HR 4805 (mimeo)
JEFFERSON, G. 1981a. 'The abominable "Ne?": a working paper exploring the phenomenon of post-response pursuit of response.' University of Manchester, Department of Sociology In: Occasional Papers 6 (A shortened version in: Schröder & Steger (Eds.), 1981, 53-89)
JEFFERSON, G. 1981b. "Caveat speaker": a preliminary exploration of shift implicative recipiency in the articulation of topic. Report to the (British) SSRC. (mimeo)
JEFFERSON,G. 1983a. 'Notes on some orderliness of overlap onset.' In:Tilburg Papers in Language and Literature 28
JEFFERSON, G. 1983b. 'Notes on a possible metric which provides for a "standard maximum" silence of approximately one second in conversation.' In: Tilburg Papers in Language and Literature 42
JEFFERSON,G. 1984. 'On a systematic deployment of the acknowledgement tokens "Yeah" and "Mm hmm".' In: Papers in Linguistics 17, 2, 1984, 197-216
JEFFERSON, G. (forthcoming). 'List construction as a task and interactional resource.' To appear in Psathas &

Frankel (eds.)
JEFFERSON, G. & J. SCHENKEIN. 1977. 'Some sequential negotiations in conversation: unexpanded and expanded versions of projected action sequences.' In: Sociology 11, 1977, 87-103. (Reprinted in Schenkein (ed.), 1978, 155-172)
KARLSSON, F. (Ed.). 1983. Papers from the seventh Scandinavian Conference of Linguistics, Vol.1. Publications no.9. Helsinki: University of Helsinki
KOMTER, M.L., 1982. 'Indringers.' In: Interdisciplinair Tijdschrift voor Taal- en Tekstwetenschap 2, 154-168
LABOV, W. 1972a. 'The transformation of experience in narrative syntax.' In: W. Labov, 1976, Language in the inner city:studies in the black English vernacular. Philadelphia: University of Pennsylvania Press
LABOV, W. 1972b. 'The isolation of contextual styles.' In: W. Labov, 1976, Sociolinguistic patterns. Philadelphia: University of Pennsylvania Press
LABOV,W. 1982. 'Speech actions and reactions in personal narratives.' In: Tannen (ed.), 1982, 219-247
LABOV, W. & D. FANSHEL. 1977. Therapeutic discourse: psychotherapy as conversation. New York: Academic Press
LAVER,J. & S.HUTCHESON (Eds). 1972. Communication in Face to Face Interaction. Selected Readings. Harmondsworth: Penguin.
LEITER,K.C.W. 1980. A primer on ethnomethodology. Oxford: Oxford University Press
LEVINSON, S.C. 1979. 'Activity types and language.' In: Linguistics 17, 5/6, 1979, 365-399
LEVINSON,S.C. 1981. 'The essential inadequacies of speech act models of dialogue.' In: Parret et al.(eds.), 1981, 473-492
LEVINSON, S.C. 1983. Pragmatics. Cambridge: Cambridge UP
LOCAL, J. & J. KELLY. 1986. 'Projection and 'silences: notes on phonetic and conversational structure.' In: Human Studies 9, 2/3, 1986, 185-204
LYNCH, M. 1979. Art and artifact in laboratory science. A study of shop work and shop talk in a research laboratory. London: Routledge & Kegan Paul
LYONS, J. 1977. Semantics. Cambridge: Cambridge U.P.
MCKINNEY, J.C. & E. TIRYAKIAN (Eds.) 1970. Theoretical sociology, perspectives and developments. New York: Appleton-Century-Crofts
MCNALL, S.G. & G.N.HOWE (Eds.) 1980. Current perspectives in social theory Vol 1. Greenwich CT: JAI Press
MAYNARD, D.W. 1980. 'Placement of topic changes in conversation.' In: Semiotica 30, 3/4, 1980, 263-290
MAYNARD, D.W. & T.P. WILSON. 1980. 'On the reification of social structure.' In: McNall & Howe (eds.). 1980
MEHAN, H. 1979. Learning lessons: social organization

in the classroom. Cambridge Mass.: Harvard U.P.
MEHAN, H. & H. WOOD 1975. The reality of ethnomethodology. New York: Wiley
MERRITT, M. 1976. 'On questions following questions (in service encounters).' In: Language in Society 5, 3, 1976, 315-357
NIEHAUS, E. 1986. 'De Markering door middel van partikels van de relationele funkties in de taalhandeling VERZOEKEN (AUFFORDERN) in Nederlands, Interlanguage, Duits.' In: Interdisciplinair Tijdschrift voor Taal- en Tekstwetenschap 6, 2, 1986, 169-178
PARRET, H., M. SBISÀ & J. VERSCHUREN (Eds). 1981. Possibilities and limitations of pragmatics: Proceedings of the Conference on Pragmatics, Urbino, July 8-14,1979. Amsterdam: Benjamins
POMERANTZ, A. 1978. 'Compliment responses: notes on the co-operation of multiple constraints.' In: Schenkein (ed), 79-112
POMERANTZ,A. 1980. 'Telling my side: "limited access" as a "fishing" device.' In: Sociological Inquiry 50, 3/4, 186-198
POMERANTZ, A. 1984a. 'Agreeing and disagreeing with assessments: some features of preferred/dispreferred turn shapes.' In: Atkinson & Heritage (eds.). 1984, 57-101
POMERANTZ, A. 1984b. 'Pursuing a response.' In: Atkinson & Heritage (eds.). 1984, 152-164
PRIDE, J.B. & J. HOLMES (Eds.) 1972 Sociolinguistics. Harmondsworth: Penguin
PSATHAS, G. (Ed.). 1979. Everyday language: studies in ethnomethodology. New York: Irvington
PSATHAS, G.K. & R. FRANKEL (Eds.) (forthcoming) Interaction competence. New York: Erlbaum
QUASTHOFF, U. (Ed.) 1978. Sprachstruktur-Sozialstruktur. Zur linguistische Theorienbildung. Kronberg: Scriptor
RADEMAKER, L. & H. BERGMAN (Eds.). 1977. Sociologische Stromingen. Utrecht, Antwerpen: Spectrum
SACKS, H. 1964-1972. Unpublished Lecture Notes. Department of Sociology, University of California, Irvine. [Transcribed and edited by Gail Jefferson]
SACKS,H. 1972a 'A initial investigation of the usability of conversational data for doing sociology' In: Sudnow (ed.). 1972, 31-74
SACKS, H. 1972b. 'On the analysability of stories by children'. In: Gumperz & Hymes (eds.). 1972, 325-345
SACKS, H. 1973. On the preferences for agreement and contiguity in sequences in conversation. Paper presented at the Summer Institute of Linguistics, Ann Arbor
SACKS, H. 1978 'Some technical considerations of a dirty joke.' In: Schenkein (ed) 1978, 249-269. [edited by G. Jefferson from unpublished lectures:Fall 1971, L 9-12]

SACKS, H. 1984a. 'Notes on methodology.' In: Atkinson & Heritage (eds.), 1984, 21-27. [edited by G. Jefferson from various unpublished lectures]
SACKS,H. 1985. 'The inference-making machine: notes on observability.' In:van Dijk (ed), 1985, 13-22. [edited by G.Jefferson from Lectures 1 and 11, Winter 1964-Spring 1965]
SACKS,H., **E.A.SCHEGLOFF** & **G.JEFFERSON**. 1974. 'A simplest systematics for the organization of turn taking for conversation.' In:Language 50,1974, 696-735 (a slightly revised version in Schenkein (ed.), 1978, 7-55)
SACKS, H. & E.A. **SCHEGLOFF** 1979. 'Two preferences in the organization of reference to persons in conversation and their interaction.' In: Psathas (ed.), 1979, 15-21
SANGERS, P. 1985. Conversatie analyse. Tweede assertie: agreement-disagreement. Werkstuk Katholieke Hogeschool Tilburg
SANTJER, M. 1985. "Topic change": hoe markeren sprekers een nieuw onderwerp?. Werkstuk Katholieke Hogeschool Tilburg
SCHANK, R.C. & R. ABELSON. 1977. Scripts, plans, goals and understanding. Hillsdale, NJ.: Lawrence Erlbaum
SCHEGLOFF,E.A. 1967. The first five seconds. The social organization of conversational openings. Unpubl. Ph.D. Dissertation, University of California, Berkeley
SCHEGLOFF, E.A. 1968. 'Sequencing in conversational openings.' In: American Anthropologist 70, 1968, 1075-1095. (Reprinted in Laver & Hutcheson (eds.), 1972, 374-405)
SCHEGLOFF,E.A. 1972 'Notes on a conversational practice: formulating place.' In: Sudnow (ed.), 1972, 75-119
SCHEGLOFF,E.A. 1979. 'Identification and recognition in telephone conversation openings.' In: Psathas (ed.), 1979, 23-78
SCHEGLOFF, E.A. 1980. 'Preliminaries to preliminaries: "Can I ask you a question?".' In: Sociological Inquiry 50, 1980, 104-152
SCHEGLOFF, E.A. 1982. 'Discourse as an interactional achievement: some uses of 'Uh huh' and other things that come between sentences.' In: Tannen (ed.), 1982, 71-93
SCHEGLOFF,E.A. 1984. 'On some questions and ambiguities in conversation.' In: Atkinson & Heritage (eds.), 1984, 28-52
SCHEGLOFF, E.A. 1986a. 'The routine as achievement.'In: Human Studies 9, 1986, 2/3
SCHEGLOFF, E.A. (forthcoming).'Between macro and micro: contexts and other connections.'To appear in Alexander et al.
SCHEGLOFF, E. & H. SACKS. 1973. 'Opening up closings.'

In: Semiotica 8, 1973, 289-327. Republished in (and quoted from) Turner (ed.), 1974, 233-264.
SCHENKEIN, J.N. (Ed.). 1978. Studies in the organization of conversational interaction. New York:Academic Press
SCHRÖDER, P. & H. STEGER (Eds.). 1981. Dialogforschung. Jahrbuch 1980 des Instituts für Deutsche Sprache. Düsseldorf: Schwann
SCHUBIGER, M. 1965. 'English intonation and German modal particles:a comparative study' In: Phonetica 12, 1965, 65-84. Republished in (and quoted from) Bolinger (ed), 1972, 175-193
SCOTT, M. & S. LYMAN. 1968. 'Accounts.' In: American Sociological Review 33, 1968, 46-62
SEARLE, J. 1969. Speech acts; an essay in the philosophy of language. Cambridge: Cambridge University Press
SEARLE, J.R. 1976. 'The classification of illocutionary acts.' In: Language in Society 5, 1, 1976, 1-24
SEVERINSON EKLUNDH,K. & P.LINELL 1983. 'The structure of a minimal communicative interaction.' In: Karlsson (ed.), 293-304
SINCLAIR, J.M. & R.M.COULTHARD 1975. Towards an analysis of discourse: the English used by teachers and pupils. London: Oxford University Press
SPRINGORUM, Th.P.A.F. 1982. Dialoogstructuur. Een onderzoek naar structuuraspecten van directiefdialogen. Dissertatie, Universiteit van Amsterdam
STREECK, J. 1980. 'Speech acts in interaction:a critique of Searle.' In: Discourse Processes 3, 1980, 133-153
SUDNOW, D. (Ed.). 1972. Studies in social interaction. New York: Free Press
TANNEN, D. (Ed) 1982. Analyzing discourse:text and talk. Georgetown University Round Table on Languages and Linguistics 1981. Washington DC: Georgetown U.P.
TERASAKI,A.K. 1976 Pre-announcement sequences in conversation. In: Social Sciences Working Paper 99. June, 1976 School of Social Sciences, University of California, Irvine
TURNER,R. (Ed) 1973. Ethnomethodology.Selected readings. Harmondsworth: Penguin (2nd edition, 1974)
WALD, B. 1978. 'Zur Einheitlichkeit und Einleitung von Diskurseinheiten.' In: Quasthoff (ed.), 1978, 128-150
WELLS,G., M. MONTGOMERY & M. MACLURE. 1979. 'Adult-child discourse:outline of a model of analysis.' In: Journal of Pragmatics 3, 1979, 337-380
WEIJDEMA,W. et al. 1982 Strukturen in verbale interaktie. Muiderberg: Coutinho
WEST, C. 1983. '"Ask me no questions..." An analysis of queries and replies in physician-patient dialogues.' In: Fisher & Todd (eds.), 1983, 75-106
WEYDT,H. (Ed). 1979. Die Partikeln der deutschen Sprache.

Berlin: De Gruyter
WILSON,J. 1980. 'Why answers to questions are not enough in social discourse.' In: Belfast Working Papers in Language and Linguistics 4, 4, 1980, 60-84
WILSON, T.P. 1971 'Normative and interpretive paradigms in sociology.' In: Douglas (ed.), 1973, 57-80
WILSON, T.P. 1985. Social structure and social interaction. Unpublished paper
WOOTTON, A.J. 1981. 'The management of grantings and rejections by parents in request sequences.' In:Semiotica 37, 1981, 59-89
WUNDERLICH, D. 1976. Studien zur Sprechakttheorie. Frankfurt/M: Suhrkamp

Kolibri 360 GmbH
Ferdinand-Jühlke-Straße 7
99095 Erfurt, Deutschland
produktsicherheit@kolibri360.de